P9-CFU-421

WE'RE GOING TO
NEED MORE WINE

Find
Fac

follo
tw

WE'RE GOING TO NEED MORE *wine*

STORIES THAT ARE FUNNY, COMPLICATED, AND TRUE

GABRIELLE UNION

An Imprint of WILLIAM MORROW

The names and identifying characteristics of many of the individuals featured throughout this book have been changed to protect their privacy. In some cases, composite characters have been created or timelines have been compressed, in order to further preserve privacy and to maintain narrative flow. The goal in all cases was to protect people's privacy without damaging the integrity of the story.

HarperCollins books may be purchased for educational, business, or sales promotional use. For information, please email the Special Markets Department at SPsales@harpercollins.com.

FIRST EDITION

Designed by Renata De Oliveira

Library of Congress Cataloging-in-Publication Data has been applied for.

ISBN 978-0-06-269398-3 (Hardcover)
ISBN 978-0-06-283559-8 (B&N BF Signed Edition)
ISBN 978-0-06-283561-1 (BAM Signed Edition)

17 18 19 20 21 LSC 10 9 8 7 6 5 4

I dedicate this book to those who have been humiliated and wanted to hide away forever. To those who have been broken and superglue wasn't enough to help. To those who have felt frozen in fear and shame. To those who have kept smiling as their throats were closing up. To those who thought they had all the answers but realized they were sorely ignorant. I see you. I gotchu. And to my parents, who I never understood until I became an adult who followed her heart . . . I'm sorry and I love you. I get it now.

contents

INTRODUCTION

This kind of feels like a first date.

I have that same feeling you get five minutes before you meet the other person, when you're giddy about where things might go. But also wary, because you've been on enough bad dates to know exactly how this can go awry. They order the salmon and pronounce the *l* and you're like, How the hell has my life come to this?

No pressure, but I have thought of you the whole time I've been writing this book. I have never shared these stories outside of a close circle of people, the friends you can tell all your secrets to because you know all of theirs. So I want this to be like one of those nights out with someone you can be real with. We're sitting across from each other over drinks, and we're in the middle of this ridiculous, hyperventilating laugh/cry because even I can't believe I did some of these things, foolishness that made perfect sense at the time but sounds ludicrous now. "Oh no, it gets worse," I say, taking a sip as everyone in the restaurant looks over at us losing it. These are the stories that require reinforcements. If I'm going to really get into them, we need to flag the waiter and tell him not to be a stranger and to keep pouring, because we're gonna need more wine tonight.

Thinking of you this past year, I jotted down notes, sent texts to myself, and went back to look at some of the books that meant something to me and left me better for reading them. One of the things I marked to share was a line from James Baldwin.

"The very time I thought I was lost, My dungeon shook and my chains fell off."

Baldwin was quoting a spiritual about the strength that comes from survival. I have felt lost plenty, stuck in the dungeons I was thrown into, and some I even locked myself into. I felt the chains of growing up trying to be someone I wasn't, and then living in Hollywood, a town that rewards pretending. The dungeon represents so many parts of my life and all of our lives. I don't think I'm special, or that my pain makes me unique. I've had a couple of moments—okay, months, maybe years—where the idea of disappearing and never being seen again seemed like an appealing option. I've been lucky that someone was always there to give me hope, whether it was a member of my support group at UCLA's Rape Crisis Center or my dog Bubba crawling under my bed to find me hiding from life after public humiliation. They rescued me from my dungeons, and later I had to do the work to shake off the shackles that I had put on myself. I hemmed myself in with shame, and also with the fear of not being chosen by men. I remember the moment I realized I was free, looking in a mirror and saying, "I choose my motherfucking self."

We'll get to that. Right now, I should just tell you at the outset that I have trust issues. I have to wonder if I will pay a consequence for telling my truth. We're entering a full-on relationship where I have all this hope that my words are going to be interpreted the way I intend. I don't want you to have to guess about my intentions. I want to make you laugh/cry as we tackle some big stuff. And if you don't agree with me, I want you to be able to say, "At least that bitch is honest." Oh, yeah, you should know that I cuss. You never knew that, did you? Having a publicist has served me well. Let's press on, nothing to see here.

It was terrifying putting myself back into some of the scenes you'll find here. But it was also the essential work of finding my authentic self. As I retraced the steps and missteps of my life, I began to stop avoiding memories that triggered emotional flashbacks, and I chose to embrace them as revelations. Each revealed a bread crumb that I had dropped along the way, leading me further on my path to understanding who I truly am.

Reading all these stories together, I wondered if I was really brave enough to share all of this. Then I remembered another quote I wrote down. This one comes from Carrie Fisher.

"Stay afraid, but do it anyway."

So cheers. Here's to us being afraid and doing it anyway.

one

LADIES AND GENTLEMEN, MISS PLEASANTON

It is a peculiar sensation, this double-consciousness, this sense of always looking at one's self through the eyes of others, of measuring one's soul by the tape of a world that looks on in amused contempt and pity. One ever feels his two-ness—an American, a Negro; two souls, two thoughts, two unreconciled strivings; two warring ideals in one dark body, whose dogged strength alone keeps it from being torn asunder.

—W. E. B. Du Bois, *The Souls of Black Folk*

When I was in the second grade, my parents moved us from Omaha, Nebraska, to Pleasanton, California. My parents had spent a year living in San Francisco just after they got married, and my arts-loving mother had lived for the city's culture and open spirit. So when my father announced he was getting transferred to go back to the Bay Area, she rejoiced. My mother pushed for Oakland, where we would be around other black families and still close to all that San Francisco had to offer. But my father, obsessed with keeping up with the Joneses, had bigger plans. He had a white work friend who had moved to Pleasanton, a half-hour drive and a world away from Oakland. "If it's good enough for Dave," he said, "it's good enough for us."

In Omaha, we were part of the largest African American extended family in Nebraska. In Pleasanton, we would be the chocolate chip in the cookie. My mother didn't want that for her daughters—me, my older sister, Kelly, and my younger sister, Tracy. Well, she lost that battle. Everything she feared came to pass.

The residents of Pleasanton divided themselves into housing developments. And where you lived said everything about who you were. We bought a house in Val Vista, which was working middle class with upper-middle-class goals. Val Vista was considered just below Valley Trails in the Pleasanton development caste system. But neither of those neighborhoods was nearly as good as the Meadows, across town, where they had green belts that connected all the cul-de-sacs and the streets. When you told someone where you lived, it was shorthand for the truth of your family's economic situation: good, average, or untouchable.

Since birth my family has called me Nickie, from my middle name, Monique. It took a little less than a year in Pleasanton for someone to call me nigger. It was during third-grade recess at Fairlands Elementary, and it came from Lucas. He was one of the Latino kids bused in from Commodorsky, the low-income housing development. He rode with Carmen, Lori, and Gabriel, or, as everyone called them, the Commodorsky kids. One day, Lucas decided my name made for great racist alliteration.

"Nickie's a nigger!" he said, pointing at me with a huge

smile of revelation, like he'd found me in a game of hide and seek. For one day to my face, and who knows how many days behind my back, "Nigger Nickie" caught on like wildfire. The kids chanted it, trying on the word as a threat ("Nigger!") and a question ("Nigger?"), and then as singsong: "Nig-ger Nic-kie. Nig-ger Nic-kie."

I couldn't afford to stand out like that ever again. So I became obsessed with observing the Commodorsky kids, clocking all the shit they did that everyone—meaning the white ones—made fun of. I wanted to be the exact opposite. And I was clocking the white kids, too, of course. I looked at them and thought, That's where I'm going to. And when I saw the Commodorsky kids, all I could think was, That's where I'm running from.

With every single move I made and every word I spoke, I stayed hyperalert to what I called the Black Pitfalls. What were the things that would make me appear blacker? I only ate chicken with a knife and fork, and never in front of white people. Certainly not KFC. And no fruit on a rind. You were not gonna see a toothy-grin-and-watermelon scene from me.

I had been warned, of course. My parents gave me the pep talk when I started school, the same speech all black parents give their kids: You're gonna have to be bigger, badder, better, just to be considered equal. You're gonna have to do twice as much work and you're not going to get any credit for your accomplishments or for overcoming adversity. Most black people grow accustomed to the fact that we have to excel just to be seen as existing, and this is a lesson passed down from generation to generation. You can either be Super Negro or the forgotten Negro.

It's actually very accurate advice. But the problem with putting it on a kid is that if you're not as good as—or eight times as good as—you feel like you are less than. Not just in academics or in sports: every kid cares about something and wants to receive love and praise for that particular quality or ability. You are always chasing, always worrying about being exposed as the dumb black kid. The foolish nigger. On one hand, it puts your shoulder to the wheel, so you're always pushing, working, striving. But one misstep and it's over. An A minus can feel like Hiroshima. It's catastrophic because you feel exposed. It's still an A, but what it feels like is "Dumb nigger." "You're a joke." "Of course you missed it, *nigger*." I had that fear as a kid, with every worksheet. Do you remember the timed tests with multiplication? I became psychotic about those. I would see "4 x 16 = ______" and hear my father's voice: "Bigger, badder, better." By the way, it's taking everything I have not to tell you I know the answer is 64. Which leads me to 64 being a perfect square, which leads me down the rabbit hole of listing other perfect squares . . . and who cares?

I did. This insane need to stay beyond reproach by being perfect also applied to getting a bathroom pass. Other kids would ask the teacher for one and she would say, "You've got five minutes," tapping her watch. She never gave me a time because I was the fastest piss in the West. I always timed myself—literally counting each second—because I wanted to come back with so much time left on the five-minute mental clock that she didn't even need to give me a deadline.

The following year, Tarsha Liburd showed up on the bus from Commodorsky. Her family had moved there from Oakland. She was black—described by everyone as "*so* black"—and she had these corduroys she wore all the time. Tarsha had a big, grown-up ass as a third grader, and the top of her butt would always be bursting out of those cords.

I didn't tell my mother there was another black girl at school, but she heard about it. "You better be nice to her," she said, "because they're all going to be mean to her."

Because Tarsha had become a walking, lumbering punch line of people pointing at her crack, I convinced myself that if I just ignored her, I would be doing right by her. I wouldn't join in on making fun of her—she was simply invisible to me.

At lunchtime, the girls at my table called a meeting. One girl looked right at me. "Are you going to be friends with Tarsha Liburd?"

Tarsha was sitting close by, so I quietly said, "No." But I made a face showing that the very idea was preposterous. Why would I have anything to do with that girl?

Another girl stared at me and said, loud enough for Tarsha to hear: "If you don't like Tarsha Liburd, raise your hand." And everyone put up two hands and looked at me.

I heard my mother's voice and felt Tarsha's eyes on me. I raised my hand just to my shoulder, a half-hearted vote against her.

"Well, I don't know her," I said. I waved my hand side to side by my shoulder, hoping it would be read as "waffling" to Tarsha and "above it all" to the table.

A day went by. I was in my Gifted and Talented education program, doing calligraphy, thank you very much, when a voice came over the intercom.

"Please send Nickie to the principal's office."

I naturally thought I was getting an *award*. My smug self just paused, elegantly finished my line of calligraphy, and packed my books. I waltzed to the principal's office, practicing a look of "who, me?" gratitude.

Principal McKinley, a burly Irish man with kind eyes, peered at me, taking my measure. "Nickie, did you raise your hand when asked if you don't like Tarsha Liburd?"

"No," I said. "I did this." I showed my discreet half wave. "Because, I, I, um . . ." I started to cry. Bawl. In my head, I was already four steps ahead, my mom disappointed in me for being mean to the other black girl.

Principal McKinley told me he was putting my name in the Blue Book. Which was, to my third-grade understanding, an unholy text containing the names of bad children. Teachers said it could follow you and you might not get into the college of your choice. The principal then told me that if I behaved for the rest of the year, he would have my name erased from it. But I didn't believe him. Even years later, when I was applying to colleges, there was a small part of me that wondered, Is my name still in the Blue Book?

I was the only person to get in trouble for this conversation, and it had to have come from Tarsha. I wasn't mad at her. I was very aware that I had done the wrong thing, but I also knew why I'd done it. It was survival of the fittest—*Lord of the Flies* in suburbia—and I had to eat.

Tarsha remained invisible to me through elementary school. At the time I told myself she was invisible because she just didn't have much of a personality. I know now that I was only justifying my refusal to connect with her. I was afraid to take the risk of being black by standing next to her.

FROM SECOND GRADE TO SIXTH GRADE, JODY MANNING AND I WERE NECK and neck when it came to grade point average. Her family lived in the Meadows—one of the richest neighborhoods in Pleasanton—and they just had nice stuff. Their house, in my mind, felt like a museum. It felt rich. When I was little, one of my barometers for wealth was if the family had Welch's grape juice. I noticed that all the rich kids drank it after school. The Mannings definitely had Welch's. The Unions had grape drink.

After school and at recess, we started playing *Days of Our Lives*. Everyone chose a character and we just invented scenarios. Jody Manning was Marlena, Scott Jenkins was Roman Brady, and my friend Katie was Hope. I'd like to tell you that this is where I discovered a love of acting. No. Maybe because I always had to be Abe the policeman. He was the only black guy on *Days*. Black Lexie didn't come on for a couple more years. So I was Abe the policeman.

As if it weren't enough that she got to play Marlena, Jody and her sister also always had coordinating, full Esprit outfits. And it wasn't from the Esprit outlets where you got like the sweatshirt and paired it with Garanimals trash. They were just perfect, those Mannings, and Jody set a high bar for competition in class. I remember we once did a presentation together in the sixth grade. The job was to come up with an ad campaign for a product, and we were assigned Bumble Bee tuna. I was the talent, thank you. Our catchphrase was just saying "Bumble Bee tuna" emphatically. Everyone was saying it at recess, so we got an A plus.

In case you are not already reaching for the Nerd Alert button, around this time, I started reading three newspapers a day. And that became an obsession, like times tables and square roots. I would figure out exactly down to the minute how long I could be in the shower, how long it would take me to get ready, and still have time to read the newspapers. The first two, the *Tri-Valley Herald* and the *Valley Times,* were exactly how they sound. Here's an actual headline in the *Valley Times,* which I cut out and laminated for my civics class: MEXICANS ROB THE MALL. Meanwhile, the "Mexicans" were from, like, the next town over, and they probably knocked over a Sunglass Hut.

So those papers didn't take me that long. But then I would read the *Oakland Tribune,* which was much more involved. On the rare occasion that I didn't finish, I would take whatever was left and I would go through it in my first-period class, usually an English class. If I didn't, I just couldn't focus. I honestly don't know what came first—a love of reading the newspapers, or wanting to be Super Negro, the magical special black person who has all the knowledge and is never caught out there looking ignorant. "She is so knowledgeable" is what I lived for. "That black girl is really something."

My other job was to be popular, which I approached with the same strategy as my studies. Meaning it was everything.

Sleepovers were the thing among the girls, and you had to be there or else you would be "discussed." I had all the sleepover worries preteens have about pranks and fears that I would smell by morning. But my hair was also a problem. I didn't want to go through the normal ritual that I did at home, wrapping my hair with a scarf, because it would draw attention to my blackness and therefore my difference. When in Rome, do as the white girls do. So I would put my hair in a ponytail or a bun and try to keep as still as possible all night—as we call it, "sleeping pretty." But eventually slumber takes over and you become a human being. By the time I woke up in the morning, my hair would be unruly.

"Oh my God, you look like Buckwheat!" someone invariably said, pointing to the mass of hair on my head. Eddie Murphy's *SNL* version of Buckwheat was still fresh and popular, all hair and teeth and "Ohtay!"

"Do Buckwheat!"

And I would do it. I would go into the "Buckwheat Got Shot" routine, with my hands in the air like Eddie's. Every time I said, "Ohtay," the girls would die.

Now that I was willingly their clown, the directives began.

"Act like you put your finger in a socket."

"Pretend you're a Kewpie doll."

I pulled my hair up to make it stand on end. Making them laugh gave me the illusion of agency and control. Minstrelsy makes the audience comfortable. Now that I am on the other side of it, and proud of my blackness, they wouldn't know what to do with me. People don't know what to do with you if you are not trying to assimilate.

Nevertheless, I did manage to create real, lasting friendships with other girls during this period. And we liked to have fun. We had our first kegger in seventh grade, right before school let out for summer. We were farting around in a park and we saw these older kids hide their pony keg in the bushes. We waited for them to leave, snuck over, got their pony keg, and rolled it right on over to my friend Missy Baldwin's house. None of us knew how to open it, so we hammered a screwdriver into the side until we made a hole and were able to drain the beer into a bucket.

And then we had all this beer! So we called people—meaning boys—and they biked over to Missy's house. There was just this trove of Huffys and BMXs dropped in her front yard as kids raced to the back practically shouting, *"Beer!"* The house got trashed and kids put her lawn furniture into her pool. This wasn't even at night and it was in a planned community. But her parents were hippies and were like, "Missy. Man, that's not cool."

That wouldn't have worked with my parents, but they had

no idea where I was anyway. They put in long days at their telecommunications jobs—my dad in San Jose, my mom in Oakland, both a one-hour commute away. My older sister, Kelly, who acted as if she had birthed herself, was given a very long leash, but she had a lot of responsibility, too. If anything happened, my sister had to take care of it. If I had a dentist appointment, she would have to take time off from school activities to play chauffeur. Class projects, homework—she was my Google before there was Google. In high school, she loved sports but didn't have my natural athleticism. She quickly recognized the gifts she had and segued into being a team manager and coaching youth basketball. Everything she wore was from Lerner, and she became a manager there at sixteen. There she was in her blazers with the huge shoulder pads. I idolized her, but also took her guidance and intelligence for granted.

She and Tracy, my little sister, had the caregiver-child relationship because of the eleven years between them. I was in the middle, completely under my family's radar. So I created a family of my friends. They were everything to me, and as a result, I was hardly ever home.

I only drank with friends, enjoying the game of getting the alcohol as much as drinking it. We'd steal from our parents or con older relatives into buying it for us. We used to play a drinking game called vegetable. Each person would choose a vegetable and try to say it without showing our teeth, and then we'd give someone another vegetable to say. You'd always pick something tough, like "rhubarb" or "asparagus" or "russet potatoes." If you showed your teeth—by laughing, for instance—you had to pound a Keystone Light or whatever contraband we'd gotten our hands on that evening. And it doesn't take a lot to laugh when you're drunk on cheap beer and high, which, oftentimes, we were.

But there were little matters of etiquette in these situations that reminded me of my place. When you shared a can of beer, the directive was always "Don't nigger-lip it." It meant don't get your mouth all over it.

Another common term was "nigger-rig." To nigger-rig something was to MacGyver it or fix it in a half-ass way—to wit, opening a pony keg with a screwdriver. Sometimes people would catch themselves saying "nigger" in front of me.

"Oh there's niggers and there's, you know, cool black people," they'd say to excuse it. "You're not like them."

In my English class in ninth grade, we read *The Adventures of Huckleberry Finn* aloud. The teacher made us take alternating paragraphs in order of where we sat in class. We were seated alphabetically by name, so as a "U" I was in the back of the class. Twain uses the word "nigger" exactly 219 times in the book. I would count the paragraphs to read ahead and see if there were any "niggers" in what I had to say. Each time a kid said "nigger," the whole class turned their heads to watch my response. Some turned to look at me just before they read it aloud, wincing in an apology that only made me more aware of the blackness I was trying so hard to escape. Others turned to smile as they said it, aiming "nigger" right at me.

But most times it felt like kids at my school simply forgot I was black. Perversely, I was relieved when they did. I had so completely stopped being black to these people that they could speak to me as a fellow white person.

"Nigger" wasn't the only slur slung around at the few people of color who dotted the overwhelmingly white student population.

But being so focused on my own situation, I wasn't always proficient in racist slang. Sure, I could decipher jokes about the Latino kids and the couple of Asian girls, but it took me a long time to realize people weren't calling our classmate Mehal a "kite." In Pleasanton you were either Catholic or Mormon, and Mehal was proudly Jewish. She invited us all to her bat mitzvah. Nobody went. Our belief system was "Jews killed Jesus, Jews are bad." Mehal flew the flag, and so she was out, but when we found out Eric Wadamaker was Jewish, it was like he'd had a mask ripped off at the end of *Scooby-Doo*.

"You know Waddy's a Jew?"

"Whaaaat? But he's so cool."

The pressure to assimilate infused every choice we made, no matter our race. Kids who didn't use the slurs certainly didn't speak up against classmates or parents using them. They adopted the language or they kept silent. Because to point out inequality in the town would mean Pleasanton was not perfect. And Pleasanton had to be perfect.

WHEN I WAS THIRTEEN, MY PARENTS BEGAN SENDING ME BACK TO OMAHA alone to spend summers with my mother's mother. It was at my request; my older sister was going off to college and I was looking for more freedom. As soon as the plane landed, I heard a sound like the sprinklers of California when they started up, that sharp *zzt-zzt,* but at a constant hum. It was the sound of insects. Cicadas provided the backdrop to my Omaha summers.

My grandmother brought my cousin Kenyatta to the airport to meet me that first year. A year younger than me, she was effortlessly cool. My grandmother raised Kenyatta while her mother, Aunt Carla, was in and out of jail. Grandma also raised Kenyatta's little brother. Aunt Carla was never out for more than a year and a half. She was awesome, don't get me wrong; she just had a problem with drugs. Kenyatta was very thin, like me, with really big eyes and chocolate-brown skin. Her lips literally looked like four bubbles, briefly joining on the edge of bursting. "Those lips," boys always said in admiration, making kissing faces at her.

Kenyatta gave me access to the cool black kids in the neighborhood. She had all these tough friends, some of whom had already been to juvie. They were all pretty and all having sex.

She had told her friends her cousin from California was coming, so a bunch of them waited outside Grandma's house to meet me. To them California was three things: beaches, celebrities, and gangs. They came ready to talk to me about what I had seen of the Crips and the Bloods.

"Hi there," I said, getting out of the car.

Their faces sank. It was over.

"Oh, Jesus," her friend Essence said. "Your cousin is white, Kenyatta."

"You're an Oreo," said this boy Sean.

It wasn't a surprise, but it wasn't something to get upset about. I had hoped to get off the plane and slip into a new life. Be a Janet Jackson doing Charlene on *Diff'rent Strokes,* or, my greatest wish, Lisa Bonet on *The Cosby Show.* The cool black girl that Pleasanton could never appreciate. But I was still just me. Luckily, I was under Kenyatta's protection. They could tease me, but only so much.

"Did you bring the tapes?" she asked.

"Yeah," I said, opening my carry-on to pull out two cassettes. She had asked me to tape California radio stations so her crew could press play and be transported to the beaches with the celebrities and the gangbangers.

We all went upstairs and crowded into her room, which would now also become my room. My grandmother had crammed two twin beds in there, so we all sat down. Kenyatta couldn't get that tape in her boom box fast enough.

Everyone leaned in as she pressed play. Crowded House's "Don't Dream It's Over" filled the room.

"What the fuck is this?" asked Sean.

"It's the radio back home," I said. "This is what they play in California."

"Do they play L.A. Dream Team?" asked Kenyatta. "World Class Wreckin' Cru?"

I pretended to know who they were, then remembered the radio station's tag line. "Um," I said. "They play the hits."

I'd taped 120 minutes of the Top 40 of Pleasanton. At first they gave it a chance. Heart. Whitesnake. They gave up at Tiffany.

Kenyatta put in a New Edition tape, and my heart leapt. I was obsessed with them, the few black boys who showed up on MTV. We girls bonded right there, talking about Bobby Brown leaving the group and Johnny Gill coming in. And which one of us Ralph Tresvant would pick out of a crowd.

I could hold my own talking about New Edition, but I felt real green on being black. And *everyone* was black in my grandmother's North Omaha neighborhood. Beyond New Edition, I wasn't up on *anything* when it came to being black. My grandma lived on the edge of what was considered "a bad area," and it was its own world, without white people. The way people talked about white folks when there were no white folks around was dramatically different—just as white folks spoke differently about black people when they thought black people weren't around, except in Pleasanton, where they forgot I was black because I blended in so well. I began studying my cousin Kenyatta and her friends to relearn blackness. Otherwise, I would be dismissed as "corny," which was the death kiss in Omaha. To be corny there was the equivalent of being labeled a "nerd" in Pleasanton—you could not come back from it. No boy would even consider coming near you. Being off-limits and forever friend-zoned was a given as the black girl in Pleasanton. But in Omaha, I had a shot at getting boys to like me the way I liked them. I couldn't blow it.

I earned respect pretty quickly, and I'm sure a lot of that had to do with being Kenyatta's cousin. Mostly I did it by keeping a poker face and not saying anything, no matter how surprised or confused I was by something people did or said. Nobody tried to mess with me.

I liked North Omaha from the jump—the dampness in the air, and how the sun never really shone. Somehow, though, the few white folks we saw on trips to the mall were all kind of tanned in this ruddy color that white people turn when they're overheated. Everyone just lived out on their blocks, hanging back, chilling, talking shit, flirting. Every so often, the sky would suddenly turn black and everyone would start running because there was a tornado coming. As soon as it blew by, everyone came back outside to the streets.

It was Midwest summer, when there's nothing to do. We were kids with no jobs, so every morning the conversation went like this: "Where are we gonna go today?" "What boy's house can we walk to?" "Whose parents aren't home?" "Who has a car?" Just finding somebody with a car was incredibly rare. In Pleasanton, everybody had a car. But in Omaha, people got around through what they called "jitneys": elderly people that you knew your whole life would say, "Hey, call me if you need me to get to the store. Just give me three dollars."

Teenagers even drank differently in North Omaha. It wasn't the binge drinking of mixed drinks in plastic cups, like in Pleasanton. If you were kicking back on the stoop you had a forty or a wine cooler. The penny candy store was right next to the liquor store, so when we hung out in front of the candy store, folks might have thought we were there to get candy, but we were really waiting on a mark. When you found one, you would shoulder-tap the guy. "Heeeey, can you get me a forty of Mickey's big mouth?" (Mickey's "big mouth" is a malt liquor also known as a "grenade," for the shape of the bottle it comes in.) It was never tough.

It was a very exciting time in my life, and there was a bit of danger that felt glamorous. The summer I was thirteen, crack started to show up in North Omaha. My aunt Carla also got out of jail. I saw her as effortlessly cool and admired her gift for always having guys around. She was staying with a boyfriend, even though she always had a home at my grandmother's if she needed it. The guys who she introduced me to were always really nice, and only later would you find out that so-and-so was involved in one of the largest drug busts in the history of the Midwest. Aunt Carla came over to Grandma's soon after she was sprung and saw a letter from my parents. They were sending me eighty dollars' cash a week that summer to give to my grandmother. Selfish me kept that cash, of course.

"Let me hold that eighty dollars," Aunt Carla said, "and on Friday, I'll give you three hundred dollars and we'll go to Red Lobster."

"Sure," I said, handing her the money. It was Monday, and I

knew I'd have another eighty dollars the next week, so it wasn't a big deal.

Wednesday my aunt came over again. "Give me your sizes," she said. "I wanna get you some back-to-school clothes."

"I want Guess jeans," I said, and then reeled off my sizes along with a list of additional asks.

Lo and behold, Friday came and Aunt Carla showed up in a limo, carrying shopping bags full of clothes for Kenyatta and me.

"Now let's go to Red Lobster," she said, handing me my three hundred dollars.

It was my first time in a limo. Kenyatta and I opened the windows and waved to everyone we passed on the ride to dinner. At the restaurant, we feasted—ordering the lobster and shrimp combo and eating every Cheddar Bay biscuit in sight. When we emerged rubbing our stomachs, the limo was gone.

"I only had it for the way over," Aunt Carla said, slotting a coin in the nearby pay phone as she took a drag on a cigarette. Her friend eventually showed up in a Buick, and as we started the drive home, she said, "I need to stop at Kmart. Stay in the car," she told us.

She went inside to write a few bad checks while we waited.

"You girls doing good?" said the driver.

We both nodded.

He proceeded to pull out a crack pipe and smoke up. The windows were closed, so we couldn't help but be hotboxed. We didn't feel any secondhand effects, but I would always immediately recognize that smell as an adult, traveling the country and going to clubs.

We were familiar with crack already, because our friends were dealers. We'd seen plenty of crack pipes and even watched people weigh it for parceling. North Omaha was rapidly changing, and every summer, the changes escalated. The L.A.-based dealers had begun to spread out across the country to get a piece of the local drug trade everywhere. Gang members came to North Omaha, selling a lifestyle as if they were setting up franchises. But it was all so bizarre to watch. North Omaha is made up of a bunch of families that have been there for generations. You walk down the street and somebody can identify what family you belong to by your facial features. All of a sudden here come these powerful gangs, splitting up families as kids randomly chose different gang sets.

A lot of my cousins and neighborhood kids that I'd grown up with during my summer visits, boys and girls, began to claim allegiance to L.A. gangs that they didn't know anything about. It started as a saccharine, almost Disney-like version of gang life. When I returned at fourteen, every young person was touched by some sort of criminal enterprise, with varying degrees of success. Some kids got one rock of cocaine and announced, "I'm a drug dealer." Then there were kids who as teenagers were doing, in terms of drug dealing, very well for themselves. They had their own apartments and flaunted their wealth.

At the end of the day, I didn't look at crack so negatively, because I saw our little friends making money off it. Drug dealing felt like any other job to me. I only knew young dealers and the random ones that my aunt knew. I didn't see the underbelly. The violence, the desperation, the addiction. All I knew was, I gave my aunt eighty dollars and she gave me three hundred dollars back. That was integrity. I later found out Aunt Carla asked her friend who was a booster—a shoplifter by profession, thank you—to get those school clothes for me at the mall. I didn't think less of her or those clothes. I thought Aunt Carla was smart. And

I went to Red Lobster in a limo. If someone smoked crack on the way home, that was a small price to pay for the adventure. A footnote, really. What remains is that she kept her word. In retrospect, I guess it's naïve to think this would all end well, but I saw honor among thieves.

In the midst of this, I was still Nickie, trying to get boys to like me, specifically Kevin Marshall. The summer I was fourteen, Kenyatta and I invited two boys over to my grandmother's with the promise of alcohol. Andy Easterbrook and beautiful Kevin. I was truly, madly, deeply, over the moon in love with Kevin. He was caramel colored, with green eyes, and a great athlete. He wasn't supposed to like a chocolate girl like me. And he liked me.

First order of business: coming through on that promised alcohol. Kenyatta and I decided to steal my aunt Joanne's wine coolers. This was the biggest mistake of the summer! God, if there was anybody who counted their wine coolers it was Aunt Joanne. But when you're a kid and you see two four-packs and there are boys to impress, you take one or two and say, "There's still some left." Boy, did we pay for that.

Next, we had to sneak Andy and Kevin into the house without Grandma knowing. Now, Grandma was always in her rocking chair, and she had to get out of it in order to see the door. So we knew that we would have a fighting chance to sneak the boys up the stairs while Grandma was working up enough momentum to propel her ass out of the chair. Even better, we knew she couldn't go upstairs because of her knees.

But as the wine cooler situation makes clear, Kenyatta and I were dumb as fuck. We ran in, pushing the boys in front of us and yelling, "Hi, Grandma! Bye, Grandma!" as we raced up the stairs. My grandma was slow and her knees were shit, but she wasn't deaf. She kept yelling, "Who all is in here?" because you can surely tell the difference between two sets of feet and four heading up the stairs. Especially boys racing to get alcohol.

So, Grandma simply refused to go to sleep. She got up from her chair and she sat in the couch next to the front door. She knew whoever we'd snuck in eventually had to come down because there was no bathroom upstairs. Somebody's gotta pee. Someone's gotta leave. And she was gonna be there to see it.

Of course, she also knew we were smoking weed up there. We were making this big attempt to hide it, blowing the smoke through the window screens. But you couldn't open the screens, and the mesh was so small that the smoke just stayed in the room. So our play to hide our business didn't work at all.

Between the wine coolers and the Mickey's big mouth they gallantly brought, the boys had to pee soon enough. They filled the empty bottles, but then had to go again. So then they had the bright idea to pour the bottled pee out through the screen. All that weed smoke not making it through the tiny mesh should have shown us that this was not a good idea. Between kid logic and the weed, it made perfect sense at the time. The piss just pooled in the gutter of the window. Hot urine in the windowsill—ah, the romance and brilliance of the teenage years.

When Grandma finally relented and went to bed in what felt like nine hours, the boys left.

"I know you had boys up there," she said to us the next morning. "I know you were smoking that weed."

"No we didn't," I said.

Aunt Joanne kept saying, "And I know you took my wine coolers!"

"No, we didn't," I said.

"Did Grandma take them?" offered Kenyatta.

"You know," I said, "other people come over here."

It's one of my greatest shames that some of my last memories of my grandmother when she was cognizant were just bald-faced lies. In a short while, she would have dementia and not know who I was. But I have to tell you, I would have done anything for Kevin Marshall. My parents let me go back to Omaha that Christmas, and the only reason I went was to have a chance to see Kevin Marshall and get a real kiss.

And I got it. Kevin Marshall tongue-kissed me on the corner of Forty-ninth and Fort, right by the bus stop.

I'm pretty, I thought. Kevin Marshall, this light-skinned boy with green eyes who is not supposed to find me attractive, found me pretty enough to kiss. On the level playing field of Omaha, a guy like Kevin was a huge get, having his pick of the pecking order of skin color that is in place in black and brown communities across the world. And he had picked a chocolate girl like me.

Then I thought, Maybe black boys like me.

THE NEXT SUMMER, WHEN I WAS FIFTEEN, I EASED BACK INTO MY BLACKness even more quickly. But North Omaha had changed more, too. It was no longer the Disney version of gang culture, it was real. The buzz in the air now seemed more scary than exhilarating. Boys would pick Kenyatta and me up to go for a ride, and we'd end up going over the bridge to Council Bluffs because they needed to pick up some money or deliver a package. It continually felt like the beginning of a bad movie. These were not bad people. These were regular kids who got swept up in the frenzy of having to be in a gang and do gang shit to impress each other. Drive-by shootings started happening, and kids began to get killed. Something very bad was coming.

My cousin was dating this guy named Ryan. He and his friend Lucky were always around. Lucky always had cornrows that never appeared freshly braided. They drove vintage El Caminos, restored status symbols they called "Old Schools." You saw these cars, lovingly and expensively restored by masters, and knew these guys had money. One night Ryan did a drive-by, shooting someone in the neck and paralyzing him. We saw a police sketch on the news and my grandma said, "Doesn't that look like your friend Ryan?"

"Nope," said Kenyatta.

"No way," I said, thinking, Yep, that's Ryan.

He came to the door later that night, after Grandma went to sleep. Kenyatta let him in quickly, and we sat on the steps leading upstairs. Ryan had the gun, and he placed it on the ground by his feet. We all stared at it.

"Can I hold it?" Kenyatta asked.

He picked it up by the handle and she held it, aiming away from us. She looked at it with a mixture of admiration and fear. This gun had been fired and it had paralyzed someone. The whole town was looking for Ryan, and here he was.

"Can I?" I asked.

Kenyatta handed it to me, and I held it like you would a caterpillar, with my fingers splayed out not to touch anything. It was so heavy. I thought, That's why he accidentally shot that kid. It's probably just too big a gun for him to aim.

"Can I stay here?" asked Ryan.

It hadn't occurred to me he would ask that, but it obviously had to Kenyatta, who nodded quickly. "We'll put you in the basement," she said. "Grandma won't know." And we did. For three weeks, we brought him food. Peanut butter sandwiches we made covertly, leftovers from dinner. Beer when we had it. We kept him company, talking about what was going on in the neighborhood. I watched some detective show where they accused this woman of "harboring a fugitive." I felt like I had a secret. I was protecting a good guy who made a mistake.

Police knew it was Ryan who had done the shooting, and it became clear to him that this hideout plan wouldn't last. He turned himself in. He went to prison. Lucky was killed the following summer, leading everyone to think they were the first one to say, "Guess he wasn't so lucky." Another friend got shot and had to wear a colostomy bag for the rest of his life. Kevin joined a gang, then his best friend Dennis died. A girl I knew stabbed a jitney driver rather than pay him five dollars. He lived. He'd known her since she was a baby and was able to tell police exactly where she lived, who her grandfather was, hell, who her great-grandmother was. Another boy that I thought was so cute shot up a Bronco Burgers. The mom of one of our friends decided she had to get her son out of Omaha. She sent him to Denver, and he got mixed up with gangs there. He got killed, too.

None of these people changed. The environment around them did. They were all good people who made choices that ended up having insane consequences. But their hearts never changed. They were playing roles assigned to them, the same way I did in Pleasanton.

WHEN I WOULD GO BACK TO PLEASANTON AT THE END OF THOSE Nebraska summers, I didn't share any of those stories. The kids I went to school with didn't deserve to hear them. They were mine, and I knew I could never convince my friends of the innate goodness of Kenyatta, Kevin, and Lucky, anyway. Of Ryan, even. So I would simply become the invisible black girl again. I checked my language, the cadence of my walk, and the confidence of just being in my skin. The older I got, the more resentful I became of these reentry periods. People in California noticed my attitude was different. I was quicker to anger at slights. I wouldn't play Buckwheat.

I especially struggled back home after the summer of hiding Ryan. I don't know if my older sister, Kelly, noticed, or if I just got lucky, but she took me under her wing. By then she was in college, starting out at USC before transferring to San Jose State. Immediately at USC, she found a very cool group of black friends. I was so jealous. When she got away from the house, she stopped having to be my mother-sister. She was just Kelly, and our relationship changed for the better.

When I was fifteen, she took me to a black frat party at San Jose State. It was like she gave me the keys to this kingdom of cool black people who valued education and fun. They were just worldly, and cool and dope and sexy. In the way that Omaha gave me an outlet for my Pleasanton frustration, my sister's world of college became a new outlet. I looked around at these students and saw black excellence. I met an Alpha Phi Alpha brother named Darryl, who talked to me for a long time that night. He even gave me his number. I gave him a fake number in return because I had lied about my age and this was a *man*. But I held onto that piece of paper for years.

That night made me see the either/or schism I was trapped in. Between Pleasanton and Omaha, I was caught in a dual consciousness: who I had to be when I was around my own people, and who I had to be in high school. Now, it's easy to see how caught I was in that back-and-forth mental chess match of trying to be okay in both worlds. "Two warring ideals in one dark body," as Du Bois wrote; the dark body of a young girl. Each was me, but the constant code-switching—changing my language, demeanor, and identity expression to fit in—left me exhausted.

"You were fly, dope, and amazing from birth," I would tell that girl now. "From the second you took your first breath, you were worthwhile and valid. And I'm sorry you had to wait so long to learn that for yourself."

two

SEX MISEDUCATION

In the fifth grade, the girls were all ushered into the school multipurpose room, where it was explained to us that WE COULD GET PREGNANT AT ANY MOMENT. Well, at least our period would strike any minute, which meant we could hypothetically conceive a child.

The problem is, Miss Brackett forgot to include the part about *how* we would get pregnant. She just left it at "it could just *happen*." No one was brave enough to ask questions. And if you don't know *how* you get pregnant, just that it MIGHT HAPPEN AT ANY MOMENT, it's a little scary. I would lie awake at night in my room, clutching my bed-in-a-bag twin sheets to my chin and wondering what could happen to impregnate me. If you were raised Catholic like I was, you already know from Sunday school that nothing really has to happen. You could go to sleep and wake up carrying Baby Jesus. I've seen countless paintings of the Annunciation, where Mary "accepts" the news that she is pregnant. But my favorite is Dante Gabriel Rossetti's at the Tate Britain in

London. Mary is in bed, giving the angel Gabriel a bleary-eyed look of "Are you fucking kidding me right now?"

That's how we felt. Are you kidding me with this "at any moment you could become a mom!" stuff? We lived in a primarily Catholic and Mormon town, so our moms definitely weren't chatting among themselves about periods. When any of my friends' moms talked to them, it was to simply hand them some pads. I certainly wasn't going to talk to my older sister about it, and because I could barely decode Tampax commercials, I looked for information in books. Naturally, my friends and I turned to *Are You There God? It's Me, Margaret,* Judy Blume's classic 1970 menstruation how-to, disguised as a preadolescent narrative. Among us ten- and eleven-year-olds, the book became required reading, and we ferreted out dog-eared copies from the local library, big sisters, and a few progressive mothers. Some girls, like me, just skipped to the blood pages. They'd hand me a copy and I'd fan through the pages to the good parts. Then I'd pass the wisdom on to the next girl. "Here," I'd say, pointing. "Then here."

We needed answers because it was all so scary—the idea of bleeding randomly and accepting it as natural seemed completely unnatural. After all, when you skinned your knee, you ran for a Band-Aid. "Where's the Bactine? I have to cover this!" But when it came to our periods, we were supposed to be celebratory? Like our moms would suddenly initiate us into their blood cult? This was a horror movie set in the leafy surroundings of Pleasanton Middle School.

It came for Melody first. In fifth grade, during homeroom. She bled right through her pants. She looked down in shock, the blood slowly blossoming in the crotch and back of her pants, and

Lucas, the boy who'd called me a nigger in the second grade, saw it first and reliably pounced.

"Melody is having her period!" he yelled out, disgusted and delighted. "Let's jump her!" He and a few of his lackeys hooted with laughter, while the rest of us looked on in horror and panic. Now an initiate into the blood cult of adult women, Melody, of course, COULD GET PREGNANT AT ANY MOMENT. (Where was the teacher? Don't ask. Faculty lounge? Smoke break?) After a few excruciating moments, Melody unfroze and ran screaming. No one followed her.

That included me. I felt ashamed. I was her friend, but for much of the school year, it was like being friends with a leper. Nobody else got her period for the longest time, but soon enough all the girls in fifth grade became familiar with Melody's month-to-month schedule, and when she was absent, we spoke gravely of her condition, dramatically shushing each other when a boy came within hearing range.

By seventh grade, Melody was no longer alone in her period drama, as all of us were getting picked off like flies. One of our friends would stay home from school or race to the nurse's office, and then we would know: "It came for her." No one I knew was excited about it. You looked forward to it the way you looked forward to food poisoning.

I knew that at any moment, it would be my turn to stand up and everyone would point in my direction. I remember we all wore dark colors in case it happened. I began carrying my jean jacket with me at all times, ready for the big moment. I pinned concert buttons all over it of the Top 40 stuff I loved—Stray Cats, Def Leppard, New Edition, Billy Joel—and tied it around my waist to conceal the inevitable evidence when the time came. We asked each other so many questions, because unless we'd been struck, none of us had answers. "Like, what happens? You put this pad on, and then what? You're just bleeding and sitting in it?"

I finally became a woman in a bathroom stall at Macy's, halfway through seventh grade. I was at Stoneridge Mall with a few friends. I felt a little dampness down below, started silently panicking and screaming, then whispered to my friends, "Oh my God, I think it's happening!" We speed-walked to the restroom, and my friend Becky, always prepared, handed me a pad. I went into the stall a girl and came out an adult.

When I got home, I tried to pretend as if nothing had happened. I balled up my bloody underwear and jeans and stuffed them deep in the closet of the bathroom I shared with my older sister, Kelly. I felt cramped and sore, but I just didn't want to have the mortifying "talk" with anyone. I don't know why I didn't throw the clothes away. I guess it felt wasteful? Kid logic is just dumb. Weeks later, my mom found them while cleaning the house.

"I found your . . ." She paused. "Soiled underwear." Ugh, to this day, the word "soiled" still makes me cringe. She handed me some pads—offering no instructions, no sitting on the couch and patting the cushion next to her—and that was that.

But I kept worrying about my next period, and I was terrified of being humiliated at school. Every month was a guessing game. "When will it happen? Will everyone find out? Will guys try to jump me and make me pregnant?" At first, I didn't know how to use the pads, and for a full year I continually had accidents because my pads were riding high. Not only did I not know how pads worked, I didn't understand how my vagina worked, either. And that's because, dear reader, I thought my clitoris was my vagina.

I started masturbating early, at age five or six. So I knew where the fun was. I knew where my clitoris was. My vagina? Not so much. I'd lived my life thinking, Of course sex is painful, because it's where you pee from! And of course childbirth is painful, because you pee out a baby! Even though I'd seen a number of anatomy diagrams, I knew where I masturbated, so I assumed that was my vagina.

I only discovered my vagina in the eighth grade, after a year of accidents. My girlfriend Danielle—Big D—and I were swimming at a local sports complex called AVAC, short for Amador Valley Athletic Club, and of course I got my period. In the water, I noticed a wispy trail of blood. It was coming from me. It was especially mortifying because AVAC was as fancy as a country club, with the best of everything. I frantically climbed out of the pool with Big D following, and locked myself in a bathroom. She talked to me through the door.

"Nick, it's okay," Big D said, concern in her voice but cool as ever. She had a bookie dad and was never prudish like most of the other girls I knew then.

"I have to go home!" I said, frantically.

"Oh, just put in a tampon," said Big D.

"I'm not a whore!" I shrieked. We just assumed tampons made you break your hymen, so if you used them instead of pads, you were no longer a virgin. And at that stage, if you weren't a virgin in Pleasanton, you were considered a whore.

"What?" said Big D. The record scratched.

"I've never used one," I whispered.

"Open the door," she said, and I did, but just a crack. She passed me a plastic-wrapped cylinder, and I took it from her, grateful.

"Now lay on the floor," I heard her voice say, coaching me through it. "Put your knees up, and just slowly put it in."

I did as commanded, laying out my plush AVAC towel and trying to put the tampon in what I thought was my vagina. "It's too big," I said.

"What?"

"It's too big."

"Let me in."

I unlocked the door. She came in, like the straight man in a screwball comedy.

"Where are you trying to put it?" she asked.

I was trying to put a tampon in my urethra.

"Um, that's not your vagina," Big D explained, slowly.

I let that sit for a beat.

"What?" I said, as casually as I possibly could.

Now I see *That's Not Your Vagina* being a great title for this little one-act play, but then I didn't see the humor.

So there we were, on the floor of a bathroom at AVAC, and Big D just slid that tampon right on up so fast I didn't think quickly enough to be freaked out. And I was all, "Where are you going?" as if she was doing a Jacques Cousteau deep dive. And she's going down. And I was like, "There's something more down there? What an amazing discovery!" Finding my vagina was a moment of "Interesting. Did. Not. Know. That." Big D was exactly the friend I needed to get me through the moment as quickly as possible. We never once spoke of it again until we were adults, not out of shame, but from a sense of "What happens in an AVAC bathroom stays in an AVAC bathroom." Only recently, when I brought it up to her, did it seem even remotely nuts.

But how was I supposed to know where my vagina was? From a young age, most girls are not given the most basic information about their bodies. And we grow into smart women who often don't go to doctors on a regular basis because we are too busy putting others in our lives first, and don't share personal medical information with each other, either. People talk about our bodies solely as reproductive systems, and we remain just as clueless as The Virgin Mary's learning she was but a vessel for something greater.

THANK GOD FOR JUDY BLUME, BECAUSE AT LEAST SHE ARMED ME WITH THE basic facts of menstruation. Nowadays, girls can Wikipedia everything—or more likely, study porn clips online.

But back then, all we had was Judy Blume. She also gifted us with *Forever*. We all knew and loved *Forever,* because it had the Sex Scene. And outside of porn (which was damn hard to procure in those pre-Internet days), *Forever* was the only depiction of sex we had ever seen. High school senior Katherine meets fellow student Michael, who nicknames his penis "Ralph" and teaches her how to rub one out, before they go "all the way" in his sister's bedroom.

We were smart enough to know that *Forever*—not the cheesy VHS porn tapes that my trusty friend Becky had discovered in her parents' room—taught us the more accurate portrait of how sex would unfold in our own lives. (Thank you, Judy!) *Forever* gave us the truth. It was about wanting to have sex, preparing to have sex, having sex, and what happens afterward. Judy Blume was our tutor.

During our freshman year, my friend Julie had sex at a house party with a boy she liked. They had planned to do it, but both were too fearful to go buy condoms. He told her he had a plan, so just before the big deed, he pulled out a plastic baggie. You read that right. A Ziploc.

A month or so later, a bunch of us were hanging out on one of the school lawns. None of us wanted to just go home and be bored, so we decided to be bored together. We were talking about how we couldn't wait for summer when Julie started crying. She leaned forward into the circle.

"I think I'm pregnant," she whispered.

We sort of fell into her, muffling her cries. I asked her twice if she was sure. It was such a stupid question, but I didn't want what she was saying to be true. My friend Barbara instead snapped into action. She was always very advanced and finger-snapping efficient with her asymmetrical bob and mod clothes.

"Okay, how much money do you have?" she said.

Julie shrugged.

"Okay," she said, looking at us all. "How much money do *we* have?"

Barbara said we needed about $350. That's what she decided was the going rate for an abortion.

Over the next couple of days, like some very special *Magic School Bus* episode, we all, a bunch of fourteen- and fifteen-year-olds, went to our parents to make a bunch of fake requests for money to buy new uniforms or to go on nonexistent field trips. In a couple of days, we got $350. The next hurdle was scheduling the abortion within the confines of the school day. To accomplish this, the lot of us cut class to go to the Planned Parenthood in Pleasanton. There was a lone protester outside. She wasn't crazy, as far as protesters go, but it was strangely terrifying. She had a sign and was just there, staring at a bunch of teenagers who didn't want anyone to see us.

Imagine five terrified fourteen- and fifteen-year-old girls sitting in a waiting room, hugging our backpacks. There was a basket of condoms on a little side table by the door. As we waited for Julie, I was eyeing those condoms. And sitting in a Planned Parenthood waiting for my friend's abortion to be over, I was still afraid of what the people working there would think if they saw me taking a condom.

Julie came out and we all hugged her. She didn't cry, she just wanted to get on with her life. She led the way out the door, walking fast and with her eyes focused forward. I trailed behind, and in one fell swoop I dumped the entire basket of condoms into my bag.

No one called shotgun. We let Julie sit in the passenger seat. As soon as the car doors closed, I opened my bag to show everyone the condoms.

"Everyone take some," I ordered.

They wouldn't. Everyone was afraid of getting caught by their parents with condoms.

"Fine," I said. "I'll hold them. But come to me, okay?"

That's how it went. I became the condom dispensary, bringing them to school and to parties whenever I got the heads-up. Adults weren't looking out for us. They assumed that we knew we could get pregnant and wouldn't risk it by actually having sex. But even when you know better, it doesn't mean you're going to do better. That's a lie parents tell themselves so they don't have to admit their kids have sex. And they do. They will either live with fear and baggies and abortions, or live with knowledge and condoms.

My dad found my stash, of course, and flipped out.

"They're for my friends," I screamed. That didn't help. I used the "What were you doing snooping in my room?" tactic, which actually worked for once. I think he was terrified.

These days, kids are mostly just honest with adults, which is just weird. I recently met a young woman in a teen empowerment seminar. "I told him I wanted to suck his dick so I sucked his dick," she said. "It's no big deal."

Um, yeah . . . No?

Now, when I try to talk to our boys or I talk to young girls, here's what I say:

"Are you ready to own your sexuality in a way that you can experience pleasure as well as give it? And be truly grown-up about it?"

But what kids are doing now, the way they process it and act on it, is so different. They would probably read *Forever* and it would be so pedestrian to them. "What kind of baby-book bullshit is this?"

But I see their "raw honesty" and I raise them.

"If you're such good friends that you gave him a blow job," I asked that one girl, "did he eat your pussy?"

"No," she said, looking at her friends.

"Well, make sure he does that next time."

"Okay."

"And then have him eat your ass," I said, "and see where that goes."

"Whoa."

"It's called reciprocation. Otherwise, it's a very unequal friendship. And I wouldn't want that kind of friendship. If you're gonna do it, then shit, really do it."

I WANT PEOPLE TO MAKE INFORMED, JOYFUL CHOICES ABOUT SEX. BEcause I love sex. In the heyday of my twenties and thirties, I loved the variety. Now that I am married, I am in a monogamous relationship. But I used to think monogamy was for suckers who didn't have options. "Some choose monogamy," I would say, "but most people have it foisted upon them."

I just didn't see the point back then. I did, however, see the point in *publicly* declaring oneself to be in a monogamous relationship. It was never lost on me that society thinks a woman should be allotted one dick to use and she should be happy with it for the rest of her life. But I always saw sex as something to be enjoyed. Repeatedly. With as many different partners as possible.

In interviews I am often asked what sage advice I have to offer young women. I admit the advice I give in *Redbook* is different than what I tell people over drinks. There is a gorgeous, perfect, talented young actress who I talked to at a party a few weeks ago.

"Look, you can't take your pussy with you," I said. "Use it. Enjoy it. Fuck, fuck, fuck, until you run out of dicks. Travel to other countries and have sex. Explore the full range of everything, and feel zero shame. Don't let society's narrow scope about what they think you should do with your vagina determine what you do with your vagina."

As I talked, the look on her face was the slow-clap moment in movies. There was the beginning of the realization that I was really saying this, then the rapturous joy of a huge smile as she knew I meant every word. Enough with teaching people to pretend that sex is only for procreation and only in the missionary position and only upon taking the marital oath. If you're having consensual sex with another adult, enjoy it.

So repeat after me: I resolve to embrace my sexuality and my freedom to do with my body parts as I see fit. And I will learn about my body so I can take care of it and get the pleasure I deserve. I will share that information with anyone and everyone, and not police the usage of any vagina but my own. So help me Judy Blume.

three

BLACK GIRL BLUES

Here is a secret to talking to teenagers: they open up best when you're not sitting across the table staring at them. For the past year I have mentored a class of teens around age fourteen. I find they share the most about what's going on in their lives when we're taking a walk. Recently, I took them out on a particularly gorgeous, sunny day. As this one boy Marcus got a bit ahead of me, he did this stop-and-start fast walk, like some sort of relay race. He would stop in the shade of a tree, then sprint through the direct sunlight to stand at the next tree.

"What are you doing?" I finally asked.

"I don't want to get any blacker," said Marcus.

"You're literally running from your blackness, Marcus," I said. "You know? It's a bit much. I'm not going to win any mentoring awards if you keep this up."

I checked in on him at lunch—the other secret to getting teenagers to talk is food. He explained that the relay race was all about girls. The girls he considered the hottest in school only liked the guys who look like Nordic princes. And that's not him.

"You're perfect," I said. "Look at my husband. He is *not* light skinned, and he has not exactly lacked for female attention. So many girls are gonna love you exactly the way you are. I'm not light."

"You get lighter sometimes," said Marcus. "I've noticed."

I scoffed. "If you want to stay inside on a soundstage with no windows for months on end," I said, "you too can look jaundiced. It's because I work inside."

"Yeah, well. It's possible then. So I'm just gonna stay out of the sun."

This kid I'm supposed to be mentoring had been sold the same ideal I had when I was young. I too went through periods where I stayed in the shade. I was obsessed with putting on sunblock, and in late summer I would insist on showing people my tan lines. "Look, this is my original color," I would say, proffering my shoulder to a white girl. "Look how light I am." I was really saying, "I have a chance to get back to that shade, so please excuse my current darkness."

I learned to apologize for my very skin at an early age. You know how you tell little girls, even at their most awkward stages, "You're so pretty" or "You're a princess"? My family played none of those games. The collective consensus was, "Oof, this one."

I was so thin that I looked like a black daddy longlegs spider with buckteeth. This is not overly earnest, false-humility celebrity speak, I swear. In case I didn't know that, the world presented a relentless barrage of images and comments making it clear to me and all my peers that most of us would never get within spitting distance of classic beauty. But I thought that at least my parents should think I was cute. When they would gather my sisters and me for a family photo, they would check each face for perfection. There was always a pause when they got to me. "Ah, Nickie, what a personality you have. You are *funny*."

In my family, light skin was the standard of beauty. This was true both in my dad's family, who were all dark-skinned, and my mom's family, who were very light. My mom was the most beautiful woman in the world to me—and I looked nothing like her.

With my dad, I simply wasn't his version of pretty. His ideal is very specific: short, light skin, long hair. I checked none of the above. Of my sisters, I looked the most like my father, and I think he wanted no part of that. As for my mother, only now do I understand that she made a decision to never praise my looks because she grew up being told her looks would be enough. They weren't. Young Theresa Glass was encouraged to build a foundation on the flower of her beauty and simply trust that it would remain in bloom long enough to win the security of a good man. Her thoughts on the books she read voraciously would only spoil the moment. "Shh," they said. "Just be pretty. When you get a man, talk all you want."

So my mom was the nineteen-year-old virgin who married the first guy who said he loved her. And by the time she had me, she'd realized that marriage was *not* the end-all. He didn't want to hear her thoughts, either. Looks had gotten her no-fucking-where.

I couldn't lighten my skin to be considered beautiful like her, but I thought that if I fixed my hair, I had more of a fighting chance at being told I was pretty. At age eight, I begged my Afro-loving mother to let me start straightening my hair with relaxer, which some called *crainy crack*. Twice a month on Saturdays, she begrudgingly took my sisters and me on the hour-long drive from Pleasanton to my cousin's salon in Stockton for the "taming" of my hair.

My mother had rocked an Angela Davis Afro in the seventies and did not approve of these trips to the salon. Yet she repeatedly caved to our demands that we straighten our hair, a political act of surrender on her part, or simply maternal fatigue. Either way, my desire to be seen and validated by my white peers when it came to my hair had the power to override her beliefs as a mother.

I cut out pictures from magazines to show my cousin what I wanted. If I was the Before, the straight-haired, light-skinned women in these pictures could be my happily ever After. One day when I was twelve, I brought a picture of Troy Beyer, the biracial actress who played Diahann Carroll's daughter on *Dynasty*. She was basically Halle Berry before there was Halle. I didn't even know that she was biracial, and I didn't know what work went into making her gorgeous straight hair fall so effortlessly around her light-skinned face. I just wanted to be that kind of black girl.

"This is what I want," I said.

My cousin looked confused, but shrugged and went to work. The deal with relaxer was that it was usually left on for about fifteen minutes to straighten hair. It's a harsh chemical, and the way I understood it was that no matter how much it itched or burned, the more I could stand it, the better. If fifteen minutes means it's working, then thirty minutes means I'm closer to glory. At thirty-five minutes I might turn white!

But the other thing with relaxers is that the hairdresser has to rely on you telling them when the chemicals start to burn. So if you're saying, "I'm good, I'm fine," they're all, "Shit, leave it on, then."

The burn is incredible, let me tell you. You start to squirm around in your seat. You're chair dancing—because your head feels like it's on fire. Eventually, you have to give in because you can't take it anymore. Not this time. In my world, if there were degrees of "good blackness," the best black girl was light skinned with straight hair and light eyes. I don't have light eyes and I don't have light skin, but at least I could get in the game if my hair was straight. No pain, no gain.

This day I was going to break my record. I would withstand any temporary pain to finally be pretty.

"You good?" my cousin said about fifteen minutes in.

I nodded. I wasn't. It didn't matter.

A few more minutes went by. I could feel the chemicals searing my scalp. I closed my eyes and gritted my teeth. I told myself this pain was only temporary. When people at school saw me, I would be so grateful and proud of my strength. Every single minute counted.

"You good?" she said again.

I nodded. Finally, I began to bawl, then weep, then scream. My cousin raced me to the bowl to rinse me out.

"Dammit, why didn't you tell me?" I ended up with lesions on my scalp where the relaxer gave me chemical burns. I was willing to disfigure myself in order to be deemed "presentable" and "pretty." To be truly seen. At twelve, I had not been once called pretty. Not by friends, not by my family, and certainly not by boys. My friends all had people checking them out and had their isn't-that-cute elementary school boyfriends. I was completely and utterly alone and invisible.

What was it like for my mother to sit there for hours upon hours, watching these black girls she wanted to raise to be proud black women become seduced by assimilation? And then to see her child screaming and squirming with open sores on her scalp because she wanted her hair to be as soft and silky as possible. My hair turned out like that of any other black girl with a tight curl pattern who'd gotten their hair relaxed and styled: medium length, slightly bumped under, except with lesions that would later scab.

Even after I was burned, with each trip to my cousin's salon, I carried with me the hope that this would be the week I was going to look like the pictures. That misguided goal remained unattainable, of course, but I could always tell the difference in the way people treated me when I came fresh from getting my hair done professionally.

"Oh my God, your hair looks so straight."

"Your hair looks so nice that way!"

Translation: You look prettier the closer you get to white. Keep trying.

If I didn't have my hair done professionally for school picture day, I didn't want to give out the prints when they arrived. There are years where my school photo is simply missing from the albums because they were given to me to take home. If I didn't look within a mile of what I thought of as "okay," I just didn't give the photos to my mother. I was not going to give her the opportunity to hand that eight-by-ten glossy to my grandmother so she could frame it next to photos of my cousins who had lighter skin and straight hair.

I would tear the photos into pieces, scattering images of myself in different garbage cans to eliminate even the chance of piecing my ugliness together. "No," I said to myself, "you're not gonna document this fuckery."

BECAUSE I'VE DONE SO MANY BLACK FILM PRODUCTIONS, HAIR HAS NOT always been the focal point of my performance. But on white productions, it is like another actor on set with me. A problem actor. First of all, they never want to hire anyone black in hair and makeup on a white film. Hair and makeup people hire their friends, and they naturally want to believe their friend who says they can do *anything*. "Oh yeah, I can do black hair," they say. Then you show up, and you see immediately that they don't have any of the proper tools, the proper products, and you look crazy. If you ever see a black person on-screen looking nuts? I guarantee they didn't have a black person in hair and makeup.

I figured this out right away on one of my very first modeling jobs, when I was about twenty-two. It was for a big teen magazine, and they said, "Come with your hair clean."

I actually washed my hair. Now, if you ask any black performer who has been around in Hollywood for more than a minute, "Come in clean" means you come in with your hair already *done*. That way, they can't screw you up. You come in pressed, blown out, or flat-ironed. Otherwise, you're just asking for trouble.

I didn't know that. My dumb novice ass showed up for my first big modeling shoot fresh from the shower. This white woman was literally trying to round brush my hair and then use just a curling iron to get the edges straight.

"You don't look like how you looked in your modeling photos," the hairdresser said. She hair-sprayed my hair and then put heat on it. My eyes got wide. She was going to break my hair right off of my head. I said nothing and did anything but look in the mirror. I didn't have enough confidence to say, "You don't know what you're doing. Step away from my hair."

She did her damage, then leaned back to take in her efforts.

"You look beautiful!" In fact, I looked nuts. Then I had to do the shoot, and proceeded to be documented for life looking like a crazy person. It was the bad school photos all over again—but I couldn't tear up all those magazines.

When I started acting, my hairstyle determined how people saw and cast me. I played a teenager for a hundred years, so I kept a flip. That flip said "All-American Nice Girl from the Right Side of the Tracks." As I was booking more jobs and meeting more and more hair and makeup people who didn't know what they were doing, I made a choice to grow out my relaxer. Now, the trope in African American hair-story narratives is that this is when I became "woke." It's not. I grew out my relaxer because my hair was so badly damaged, it was split to the scalp. If you're on a production that does not believe in diversity in the hair and makeup trailer, it's a lot easier to let them style a weave than let them touch your real hair. I was also then getting a lot of attention from the type of black men that every black woman is supposed to covet, and a good number of those particular men had been conditioned to love long hair. These two things went hand in hand—I was being chosen and validated.

I stopped using my own hair probably after *7th Heaven,* in the nineties. I have always had very good weaves, so when I cut my weave for *Daddy's Little Girls* and *Breakin' All the Rules,* people thought I was just "crazy experimental with my hair." No, I am just crazy experimental with hair that I can purchase. After a certain point, when my natural hair was long and healthy, I just put it up in a bun. I didn't politicize my choice. It was another option, that's it.

Then, because of work, wigs became so much easier to use and offered me more flexibility. My hair is braided down underneath, and every night I pop the wig off. Sometimes I leave the set rocking my own braids like Cleo from *Set It Off*. I still wash my hair and rebraid it. Then I can pop that wig back on and go to work. The less time I have to be in hair and makeup, the better.

Still, I struggle with the questions: Does this wig mean I'm not comfortable in my blackness? If I wear my hair natural, do I somehow become more enlightened? It is interesting to see the qualities ascribed to women who wear their hair in braids or in natural hairstyles, even among black people. We have so internalized the self-hatred and the demands of assimilation that we ourselves don't know how to feel about what naturally grows out of our head.

Being in an all-black production is no guarantee that your hair won't be a source of drama. Recently, I was in one and there was pushback about getting a natural no-heat hairstyle. I thought it would be an interesting option for my character.

"Well, we want her to be like, really pretty . . ."

"Honey, my face is where the action is," I said. "Natural hair *is* pretty, but my face is the moneymaker."

When I did *Top Five* with Chris Rock, the character needed to have her hair blond. I knew that if there were paparazzi photos from the set posted online, it would start an avalanche of "Gabrielle Wants to Be White" blog posts. So I got in front of it and posted a selfie on Instagram captioned, "New day, new job . . . new do." I thought the message was clear: This is for a role. Don't come at me with your @'s. I pressed Share and that was that.

Well, that didn't work. "Why did you do this?" was written over and over again. I felt judged. A person I never met wrote, "What happened to my baby?" I felt completely outside myself in a way that was not comfortable at all. There is an idea that if you choose to have blond hair as a black woman, you are morally deficient. I didn't just have to read it on social media, I could *feel* it in interactions I had away from the set.

It would be naïve of me to say that hair is just an accessory. I recognize that black hair has been politicized, and not by us. We have since reclaimed that politicization. We have ascribed certain characteristics to people who rock a natural look versus weaves and wigs. If you choose to have natural hair, or even to promote the *idea* of natural hair, you are somehow a better black person than someone with a weave or someone who straightens their hair. You have transcended pettiness and escaped the bonds of self-esteem issues. But I have traveled around the world and I know this to be true: there are assholes who wear natural hair, and assholes who wear weaves. Your hair is not going to determine or even influence what kind of person you are.

GROWING UP, I WAS ALSO OBSESSED WITH MY NOSE—AND NOSE JOBS. I still kind of am. I first became aware of rhinoplasty when people started making fun of Michael Jackson getting his first big one. I was on the playground and a kid asked, "How does Michael Jackson pick his nose?"

He didn't wait for me to answer. "From a catalog!" he yelled.

I paused. "Wait, that's a thing? I don't have to live with this nose if I don't want it?" It wasn't just Michael. Growing up, it felt like every black star, people who you thought were beyond perfect the way they were, changed their nose. The successful people, who used to have noses like you, suddenly didn't. It only made me more self-conscious. I would stare into the mirror, thinking about how as soon as these people got the chance to fix their mess of a nose, they did.

Like them, I wanted a finer, more European nose. I used to call my nose the Berenstain Bear nose, because I thought it looked exactly like the noses on that family of cartoon bears. As a kid I tried the old clothespin trick. I would walk around my house with my nose pinched in a clothespin, hoping it would miraculously reshape my nose. I had a method, attaching it just so and mouth-breathing while I did my homework. It didn't work.

There was a whole period of time in high school where I would do this weird thing with my face to create the illusion that my nose was thinner. I'd curl my upper lip under itself and do a creepy smile to pull down my nasal folds. I thought I was a nasal illusionist, but I ended up looking like Jim Carrey's Fire Marshall Bill on *In Living Color*.

The reality is that growing up in Pleasanton and coming up in Hollywood, nobody ever said one word about my nose. I imagined people talking about my nose, but it was really just noise that originated in my own mind. People have since accused me of having a nose job, however, which made me even more convinced that people thought that I had a nose I should want to fix.

So here is the truth: I have never had a nose job. I am, in fact, the Fugitive of nose jobs. Like Dr. Richard Kimble, blamed for killing his wife, I too stand accused of a crime I didn't commit. It's a constant on social media. Catch me in the right light, or after a contouring makeup session some might deem aggressive, and the comments section lights up. "Nose job." "Fillers." "She fucked up her face." The next day I'll post another shot with my nose fully present and accounted for and people will literally say, "She let the fillers wear off." It takes everything I have not to write these people and say, "Do you have any idea how fillers work?"

Okay, I will admit I have researched. I have even fantasized about putting myself in the able hands of Dr. Raj Kanodia, Beverly Hills sculptor to the stars. A white friend went to Dr. Raj, and afterward I took her chin in my hand, literally holding her face to the light like it was a beautiful work of art. We actresses talk and share secrets, so I know people who feel they owe their careers to his work. But that won't be me. I can't even get the slightest tweak, because I will be slammed. I am stuck getting all the flack for a nose job without any of the benefits.

Maybe one day, when I'm a real grown-up, I will wear my hair natural and I won't contour my nose. Hell, I'll just be me. And hopefully people will accept me the way I am.

four

THE BALLAD OF NICKIE AND LITTLE SCREW

Here I am, three decades later, and it is as if I am seeing him for the first time. He just suddenly appeared, striding across the massive fields at Sports Park. It was the summer before ninth grade, and those of us who played sports year-round hung out at the park constantly.

He wore a yellow polo shirt that matched a stripe in the plaid of his Bermuda shorts. And of course he had his baseball hat on, with sandy blond-brown hair sticking out from underneath. Now, that wouldn't be a color anyone would want. You would sit in the salon chair, take in its dullness, and say, "Get rid of this." His teeth weren't at all straight, with gaps dotting his crooked smile. Everyone else in Pleasanton got braces in elementary school—I was considered late to the game in fifth grade—so his gappy grin made him special. He walked bow-legged, a Marky Mark swagger to every watched step.

Lucy laid claim to him first. She was "the Mexican" in our group of friends. As he walked, she told us everything she knew about Billy Morrison. Everyone called him Little Screw because his older brother's nickname was Screw. Screw looked like someone had put a palm on his face and turned it counterclockwise, ever so slightly. The rumor was he'd gotten hold of a bad batch of drugs when he was a kid, and as a teenager his face just grew that way, but that was probably just a stupid rumor. Screw and Little Screw's parents had a tire store franchise and had just moved from Fremont. They were flush enough to move into the Meadows development, but saying "Fremont" in Pleasanton was an insult, so they had baggage. You heard the imaginary organ play a sudden "dunh dunnnnh" behind that phrase. There were a lot of Mexicans in Fremont, people said, and maybe even Filipinos. And poor white people. Little Screw had gone to a private Christian school before his family moved up and moved out. And over and over this is what I heard about him:

"You know . . . he had a black girlfriend . . ."

It was always whispered with an air of "*this* is how wild this guy is." I had stopped being black to these folks years ago, so it was said sotto voce for the shock of it, certainly not for my benefit. But it meant I had a chance with Billy. Little Screw might be able to like me.

As brown people, Lucy and I had heretofore been ineligible for the dating dramas of middle school. We were always "the friend." The town was made up of Mormons and Catholics, and to this day remains deeply conservative. Lucy, at least briefly, had luck with Jeremy Morley of the Mormon Morleys, which seemed like this unbelievable coup. But mostly we were always "the friend." At the school dances, I would always have to ask somebody to dance, blurting out "JUSTASFRIENDS" before they thought I had some twisted idea. And certainly no one ever asked me. When we danced as a group and a slow dance came on, the unlucky one would end up with me. During Poison's "Every Rose Has Its Thorn" or whatever slow dance, I'd look wistfully over the guy's shoulder, suspecting he was looking at everyone else and rolling his eyes. Dancing with me was an act of charity, a Make-A-Wish mercy dance.

I didn't have a model for what I was feeling until I saw the black eunuchs from Mel Brooks's *History of the World, Part 1*. In the movie there is an extended boner joke with Gregory Hines hiding among the sexless, castrated guards allowed to be in the maidens' chambers. He fails the eunuch test while the real ones pass with flaccid colors. In my heart, I was Gregory Hines with a hard-on, but to everyone else I was the eunuch. You can be the trusted confidante or witty sidekick, there and in the mix. But remember, you don't appeal to *anybody.* Not to the whites, but also not to the very few people of color, either. The two African American boys in my grade wanted nothing to do with me. And the other two black girls steered clear of me and each other, to avoid amplifying our blackness. Because anyone brown would say, "Well, if I hang with you, then we'll become superbrown." So I was a eunuch. A social eunuch.

For all of freshman year, Billy was an electric current moving through my group of friends. We would trade Billy sightings. Someone would say they spotted him at lunch or in the hall. "What did he have on?" we would ask in response. "Was he wearing his hat?" He wasn't in any AP or honors classes, so

I would only see him at sporting events. He played baseball—because of course he didn't play soccer like every other Ken doll in Pleasanton—so we made sure to go to every game. When he played basketball, we admired the muscles of his arms and his tic of pulling his shirt away from his chest after he scored. He never looked around, never held up his arms in victory if he sank a basket. He just continued on as if he'd wandered into a pickup game that he might leave at any time.

When I would run into Billy, it was usually at the Sports Park between games. I would have my bag of softball equipment and he would be lugging his baseball equipment.

"Did you win?" he'd ask.

"Yeah," I'd say. "You?"

"Yeah."

"Cool," I'd say.

"Yeah, cool."

Walking away, I would feel high just from that brief encounter.

Billy hung out with all the athletes, but he was close friends with Mike, whose dad was the basketball coach. Mike's whole family was made up of great athletes—the sports dynasty of Pleasanton. To run afoul of any of them was social death. Billy's friendship with Mike ended abruptly one night at basketball practice, when Billy got into it with Mike's dad and told him, "Suck my balls."

And that was that.

But Billy seemed exempt from the social hierarchy. The incident just added to the legend of Little Screw. Billy was two years older than us and already driving. His car was the only freshman's car in the parking lot. He had a GMC truck. It was black with gold trim, with BILLY emblazoned on the back in tan paint. I wanted it to read BILLY AND NICKIE so badly. He was such a badass in that ride. His parents were always away, either taking an RV trip or busy with their store in Fremont, so he and his brother had more freedom than most kids. They threw huge parties, and my friends and I always went. Our parents all worked long hours, so they never really had a line on where we were or what we were doing. I routinely used the "I'm staying at so-and-so's house" line when I was really out partying. There was only one parent who cared where we really were: Alisa's mom, Trudy. You never name-dropped Alisa in any of these schemes because Trudy would go looking for her and ruin everything.

It was Lucy who lost her virginity to Billy first. I was so jealous, but I masked it. "Tell me everything," I said, as if I was happy for her. I wanted to be the one so much that I didn't even hear her describing what had gone down. I was too busy thinking, He had a black girlfriend, Lucy is Mexican . . . I have a shot. The door is clearly open.

Little Screw and Lucy didn't go out or even have sex again. He just moved on to Alice, another Mexican girl. Billy claimed her. He called Alice "my girlfriend." I had to figure out what secret pull she had. She lived near me in Val Vista, considered next-to-last in the Pleasanton development caste system. Alice was on the traveling soccer team, and she was big on wearing her warm-up pants to school, along with slides or Birkenstocks with socks. She always had a scrunchie to match her socks, usually neon pink. She would wear part of her hair up, the rest falling in curls.

A rumor went around that she was a freak in bed. "You know, she rides guys," someone told me, "and then leans back and plays with their balls." If you've never had sex, that sounds like some acrobatic Cirque du Soleil–level shit.

Everyone was having sex by this point except me. Freshman

year ended and I went to Omaha, where I at least had a chance with boys. The real test that summer was when I went to a co-ed basketball camp. The black guys there had a thing for me, though I was too focused on basketball to do anything. "You're like a white girl without the hassle," one guy told me. He meant it as a compliment, and on some level, I probably took it as one. Nonetheless, they saw me. I was a viable option.

Being the eunuch in Pleasanton, I was still in the middle of the long, long process of being Friend to Billy. I wish I could say it was strategic. The rare times he would go to some kid's bonfire, I would slide on over to him as casually as I could. Southern rock was massive then, so there was always a lot of Lynyrd Skynyrd and Allman Brothers to be heard. At every party, Steve Miller's "The Joker" was played at least twice. You'd find young Nickie, standing next to a fire, talking to a white boy in a Skynyrd T-shirt emblazoned with the Confederate flag. These young bucks, scions of upper-middle-class families, wishing they were back in Dixie. Away, away. And then there was Billy, looking as out of place as me. He was more into driving around playing Sir Mix-a-Lot. I'd hang on to every word he said. He would complain about Alice, and I would chime in, coaching from the sidelines as only a friend could do.

"Just tell her how you feel," I'd say, thinking, Just tell *me* how you feel.

They broke up, and my determination to be noticed by Billy only grew. At one of the parties at his house around November of sophomore year, Billy gave me a sign. He looked at me in such a way that I just knew.

"We should hang," he said.

I felt *invincible.*

HERE'S HOW IT WENT: ON SATURDAY, NOVEMBER 12, 1988, BILLY AND I made a plan for him to pick me up at my house after I went to a Warriors game to celebrate my little sister's birthday. I still remember the score: the Warriors beat the Portland Trail Blazers, 107–100. I borrowed my friend Danielle's light blue denim skirt, and as my parents slept upstairs and I waited for Billy to pull up in his GMC, I checked myself in the mirror roughly fifty-six times. When he finally showed, I walked out the front door and left it unlocked.

We drove to his house and he led me straight to his parents' bedroom. Remember how it felt as a kid when you went into your friends' parents' bedrooms? They just felt grand. Holy shit, I remember thinking, I'm so not supposed to be in here. We're in here and we're going to fuck.

I lay down and the panic set in. He'd already had sex with Alice, the ball-fondling sex acrobat, so in my mind I saw Alice smirking at me, always so sure of herself in those fucking soccer warm-ups, that neon scrunchie barely able to hold the glory of her hair.

In comparison, I was *so* black, I was *so* not cool, and I was *so* inexperienced.

Billy started to kiss me. My mind was racing. What if my vagina looked like a fucking dragon? I had another friend who was really into trimming and shaving her pubic hair. This same girl would even sometimes shave her vagina using a mirror. She would then brag-slash-explain to all of us using very adult words: "Well, if you don't know yourself . . ."

And I don't know myself! At all! And now Billy's going to see me and even I don't know what he's going to see. Then it occurs to me: Oh my God, he is going to have sex with black pussy.

I knew, even though I was so inexperienced, that in interracial porn there is a lot of "Give me that black pussy" talk. And I had always thought it sounded so dirty. Now I realize that in fact *I* have black pussy. Did he have sex with that black girlfriend back in Fremont? I hadn't thought about my vagina in relation to other vaginas he'd seen. And I hadn't done anything to mine in preparation. So now, I thought, he is going to see this black *Teen Wolf* pussy. It's going to look different, smell different, be different. He is going to be repulsed. And if this doesn't go well it will be because he is rejecting my black pussy.

We got under the covers and I pulled up my skirt to fumble out of my underwear, doing as inelegant a job as possible. We left our shirts on.

"I'm a virgin," I said.

He smiled. I later found out that this was his thing. He was the Deflowerer. It's not why he had sex with me, but he was known for being a lot of people's first time.

He didn't even look at my vagina. He started to put his dick in and then he looked at me, trying to gauge: "Am I killing you?" I was silent. It was uncomfortable, but it wasn't, like, crazy painful.

And then it was. I start making this bug-eyed look that I knew could not be sexy. I flashed through every book I'd ever read that included a sex scene and landed upon the words, "Look him in the eye." So I tried that. Weird. It's too much to maintain eye contact with a guy when you're sixteen years old and mortified.

He was very gentle and so determined, like he was solving a math problem. But he still hadn't laid eyes on my vagina. I was still wearing Danielle's skirt and I started to panic, because I realized that when I gave it back to her it was going to smell like sex.

She would know. Because at first you don't want anyone to know, but then you want the whole fucking world to know.

I waited for all the things I had read about to happen, while trying to mask the pain, horror, and humiliation.

It started to not hurt anymore. Maybe even feel good. And then, with a strange sound, it was over. Where was the magic? Where was the cuddling? The fireworks and the I-love-yous? *Something. Anything?*

He got up to flush the condom, and I saw his bare butt for the first time, watching that bow-legged walk across the room. He was a dude strutting around in a white Hanes tee and tube socks. I let out a contented sigh. He was just so sure of himself that it was infectious. I had just lost my virginity.

When he came back to the bed, we locked eyes, and all my newfound self-assuredness disappeared. I felt ridiculous. I felt exposed. He hadn't seen my black pussy, but did it feel different to him? Did he like it? Did he hate it? Is that why he came so fast?

He leaned on my side of the mattress.

"We're gonna have to wash these sheets."

"Huh?"

"You bled all over the sheets."

There was no sweetness. It was simply a statement of fact, like a detective at a crime scene. I got up, and I saw what he saw. It *was* a crime scene, there on those light gray sheets. The books never described it that way. The books never said there would be this much blood.

Inside, I wanted to die. In fact, I decided I *was* dying. A little of humiliation, and a little physically. I crossed some weird boundary, turned around, and found that the door had vanished behind me. I was stuck in a weird space of middle earth.

I had unleashed my black pussy on the world, and look what happened. Here's this perfect man, and I've ruined the sheets of his parents' bed. I wanted to crawl into a ball and call my best girlfriend and write it in my diary—all at once. And now I had to wait for a whole laundry cycle?

Yes, I did. We sat there in his living room, barely talking. And as we waited for the dryer to ding, I felt myself slip-sliding right back into the friend zone. I was already mourning all the flirtation, the touching, the little signals of interest.

He drove me across town, back to my house. When we finally pulled up, he jerked his head toward the car door like I didn't understand how it worked. I sat. I waited.

"Y'all right?" he said.

The car was still running.

"Yeah, yeah."

He nodded. I wanted him to kiss me the way Molly Ringwald got kissed. In my head I was screaming, "I want you to be Jake Ryan! Kiss me like that!"

He didn't.

I let myself out of the car and closed the door softly.

As I walked to my house, I pretended not to watch him drive away.

BILLY GOT BACK WITH ALICE SHORTLY AFTER WE HAD SEX.

When Billy showed interest in me, I felt myself vibrating with sexual energy. I wasn't Gregory Hines in the eunuchs' chamber anymore. What's more, people could see it. Everyone around me knew that I was a viable option. My confidence swelled—and promptly deflated when he moved on to someone else. For a few weeks, I remembered looking around, scanning the halls and classrooms for signs of other interested suitors. "Anybody else? Anybody? No?"

No. I was back to eunuch status. But now I'd had a taste. I knew what was on the other side.

I wanted a do-over. Later that school year, I got it. It was in February. Billy and I had sex on the ground outside an industrial park. I drank a Mickey's big mouth. This time, I thought, it was for real.

That one didn't do the trick either. We did have a pseudo-romance of sorts and hooked up many more times. Throughout my teens, I never dated a guy without cheating at least once with Billy. Even now, I google him. I'll be with someone from Pleasanton and he'll come up in conversation. The other person might say, "I wonder what he's . . ." and immediately it's "Hold, please," as I start typing. Or if I'm with a mutual friend from home and they have a laptop open, I direct them: "Go to his Facebook." I don't want to actually connect. I just want to be a voyeur. I want to see how his kids turned out. I want to see if they're ballsy like him.

But it doesn't matter. As many times as we hooked up, there would never be BILLY AND NICKIE painted on the back of that GMC. I was never his Chosen One.

five

OPEN HOUSE

When I was little, my mom would take me with her to open houses. We'd drive out to Oakland and San Francisco—cities she loved far more than our town of Pleasanton—and we'd wander from house to house. These were homes that we no way in hell could afford, but we toured them just to see how other people lived. People who were not us.

I was eight when we toured a huge San Francisco Victorian, all light wood and curving staircases with a bay window that actually looked out on the bay. I ran to the window to take in all the blue of the water.

"Your world is only as small as you make it, Nickie," she said.

That was the same year she took me to see Nikki Giovanni recite poetry at the Oakland Children's Museum. We sat high up in coliseum seating, listening as Nikki talked about dragonflies and strawberry patches. My mother kept nudging me into listening. "Isn't this wonderful?" she asked again and again.

Mom was always taking my sisters and me to events like this.

She loved the ballet and would take us to see *The Nutcracker* at Christmas. She would buy tickets for the Alvin Ailey dance company whenever they were in the Bay Area. On every one of these excursions, she would inevitably start talking to a stranger. My sisters and I called them Random Acts of Conversation, rolling our eyes. "Where are you from?" she would ask the rando she had found, whose existence we would then be dragged into acknowledging. "Oh, wow," she would say.

Mom was so bored and lonely in the small world of Pleasanton. When my parents moved there, my father simply stopped including her when he went out. And Cully Union, an extremely social person who could also talk to anybody—except his wife Theresa—went out a lot.

My parents both had telecommunications jobs, he at AT&T and she at Pacific Bell. Back in Nebraska, they also worked a night shift cleaning a day-care center so I could receive free care when I was little. My father was obsessed with upward mobility and after he got his BA degree from the University of Nebraska at Omaha, he later got an advanced degree going to night school. My mother was pursuing her master's at Holy Name, a Catholic college in Oakland. My dad thought that her studies would help her move up the ranks at Pacific Bell. But learning for my mother was about her love of literature. Her time at Holy Name was meaningful for her. To this day, she talks about two classmates, a Chinese American and Mexican American who took her out to try Thai food for the first time. When my father realized her higher education was in the humanities and would not result in more money for the household, he stopped funding it. He hadn't cared to know what she was studying, because Dad is always oblivious to things he isn't interested in. She never completed her master's.

Meanwhile, he was funding his second life. Around my junior year of high school, I discovered a green ATM card in a drawer. I brought it to my older sister, Kelly.

"There's a lot of money in that one," she said.

It was the card Dad used to finance his life with another woman. Kelly was aware of the reality long before I was. She had gotten a sales job with AT&T, working out of the Oakland office while my dad was in San Jose. Kelly's job took her up and down the bay, and whenever she was close to San Jose my dad would say, "Let's link up and have lunch."

But it came with the caveat, "Just let me know before you come to the office."

One day she surprised him. Dad was in a meeting in the conference room, and someone gave Kelly a folder to leave on his desk. He had a glass desktop, under which he kept several family photos. Where there was usually one photo of my mom and dad, this time there were instead several photos of my dad with another woman.

"She looked so much like Mom," Kelly told me. "But she's not Mom."

Kelly said that once she discovered the reason for the green ATM card, she would ask Dad to lend it to her—basically daring him to say no. After a while, I told him he also needed to give me the card.

"Take out twenty dollars," he'd say, expressionless.

I'd take out two hundred.

Then Kelly found the secret photo album. She always did know where to snoop, although my father didn't put much effort into hiding it. It was right under the bed, almost in plain sight. The other woman had put together an old-school family photo album of all their trips together, thick and loaded with time-stamped pictures in plastic sheaths. My sister and I examined the dates, realizing he had been lying to us for years about his whereabouts.

Kelly pointed at a photo of my father with this woman who was not our mother in front of a waterfall, wearing leis.

"February 14," I said.

"That was the conference . . ." Kelly said.

"In Parsippany!" we said together.

"You were in Kona, asshole," I said, turning to the next page.

Kelly had been right. My mother and this other woman were the *same* woman: short, light-skinned, with freckles. They each had short blond hair.

He had a type.

I started calling the green ATM cash "Hawaii money." My dad never acknowledged in any way that Kelly and I knew about the other woman or what this card was for. Life simply continued, with him feeling he still retained his full authority over us. During my senior year, my soccer team was in a tournament against our archrival Fremont. Dad loved those soccer games, sitting in the all-white audience with a megaphone, watching his daughter outrun everyone. That day, I shanked a penalty kick in Sudden Death. Game over. I looked to my dad. He put the megaphone down and wrapped his hands around his neck. His eyes bugged out and closed, his tongue lolled.

Then he stopped, looked me right in the eye and mouthed the word "Choke."

The parents to the left and right of him saw the act and laughed. He laughed with them, his chosen people.

"Fuck you!" I yelled, stomping off the field. Up until that

point, I had never sworn at my dad in my entire life. Only once did I allow myself to look back at him: his bemused expression showed the slightest bit of pride. Like, "Look at you, kiddo."

FOR THE LAST FIVE YEARS OF THEIR MARRIAGE, MY PARENTS DID NOT speak to each other. Not to say "Excuse me" in the kitchen during the morning rush, or even a reflexive "Bless you" after a sneeze. This was during my senior year of high school and into my college years. My mother slept on the couch in the living room, like a boarder. My sisters and I all led separate lives.

One morning, it looked like my mother caught a glimmer of hope. She discovered two tickets Dad had bought for the ballet. It was the kind of thing my father would never want to do, much less with his wife.

So Mom took off early from work that day, had her hair done, and bought a new outfit. It goes to show how much my mother worked, because I remember distinctly how bizarre it was to see her at home while the sun was out, in the middle of the week.

Dad came home shortly after her. She sat on the couch, pretending to read a magazine and waiting patiently as he moved about the house. She didn't let on that she knew about his ballet surprise, even though she was completely done up. I can imagine her, in her mind, practicing her surprised face.

He strode over to the side table, where the tickets were. He bent over, picked them up, and strutted out the door. My mother's face took on a faraway look. She pretended none of this humiliation had happened.

The next morning, I didn't ask him where he'd been. Inside, I felt humiliated on my mother's behalf, but on the outside, I showed the passive politeness of a fellow boarder in this house.

I CALLED RECENTLY AND I ASKED HER ABOUT THOSE TICKETS.

"You know, what I want you to know more than anything," she said, "is that everything you remember is what you remember."

After a long pause, she sighed. "The tickets," she said. "I just thought . . . perhaps."

The word hung in the miles between us. I myself say "maybe" when I don't want something to happen. I reserve "perhaps" for when I get asked about things I hope for.

"Those weren't the first tickets to something that I would have liked to go to, nor the last," she said. "I was ready, in case he, on this day, thought to take me. But I was also prepared for him not to take me."

"When did you know he was cheating?"

"I didn't," she said.

"Mom," I said.

"We never had the conversation once in our entire marriage," she said. "I wasn't looking for it. I loved my *house*. I loved the swimming pool. I loved my life with you girls. I loved having money in the bank. I loved having the creature comforts that we worked so hard for. My feeling about him was 'I'm happy, and as long as you don't disrupt that, I don't care what you do.' "

Everything you remember is what you remember.

My mother told me that on Sunday nights Dad was always out late. So she began to go out herself, something I don't remember at all. I only recall Mom waiting at home for Dad. She would leave after Tracy and I were in bed. I was probably sneaking out the same nights.

"There were a lot of live jazz places that your dad didn't go to," she said. "One of my good friends from work, her husband was in a band, and I would meet up with her."

Her girlfriends considered her bait to draw men in. "A blond black woman, I don't care if you're rail thin or four hundred pounds, you're gonna get a lot of attention," my mother told me. "And I always got a lot of attention." She never acted on it, she said, but relished the idea that she was pulling them in for the team.

"Most of the time I wouldn't run into any of your dad's friends," she said. "And most of the time it wouldn't get back to him. But sometimes it did, and that was okay, too."

He knew more than she realized. Our longtime neighbors who lived across the street, a Filipino family, socialized with Dad and the other woman. Turns out the wife was always spying on my mom. "I saw Theresa leave last night," she would narc to my dad. "Where did she go?" My dad was always Mr. Neighborly, acting like the mayor of our street, and my mom was more interested in reading a book inside than chatting in the driveway. Other couples also became complicit as they began to double-date with my father and my mother's stand-in. I guess she just seemed like a better fit for their friend Cully. They wanted Mom out.

I watched Dad try to make the ride bumpier for Mom. I could tell he hoped he could buck her off, but she was not going.

"He always was a great provider," she told me. "He made sure we had a really nice home and that my children were well taken care of."

It was, she said, a lesson from an epic fight she had had with her own mother. As a teenager, Mom worked in a hospital as a cleaner. My grandmother happened to be there one day and Mom complained about how much she hated the job.

"Shut up," my grandmother told her. "Shut your mouth and get your check. When you find a different job, then you leave. But otherwise, keep your head down, shut your mouth, and get that check."

Mom paused. "We had a good life."

THE NIGHT MY DAD FINALLY GOT HIS WISH, HE WAS HOME FROM WORK before Mom. I was visiting from UCLA. Tracy was at the house and Dad said something cruel to us girls, who knows what, and we both started crying. He left and my mother came home to the chaos of daughters in tears. Tracy screamed that Dad was mean. Mom calmed us down and eventually, we went to bed.

My mother stood alone in the kitchen. My father had left her a note saying that he wouldn't be home until late. He had spelled her name wrong: "Teresa." They'd been married nearly thirty years.

He didn't know that my mother had called the bank that day. She'd tried to pay their property taxes and the check bounced. Their bank account was overdrawn. She remembered the night before, when my father announced that he wasn't paying for braces for my little sister. "She doesn't really need them," he'd said.

He had just been on another business trip.

Something in my mother finally broke.

She turned the note over and took a pen.

"I am leaving you," she wrote.

She went to her brother's house. My uncle was living in Fremont with a roommate, and then my mom became his roommate. Tracy stayed with my dad and finished high school, but there was a point when she was living with my mom in Fremont and going to high school in Pleasanton.

My mom insists she only found out about the affair when she met someone who knew Dad from AT&T.

"You have a beautiful home," she said.

"You've been to my house?"

"Yes," she said. "Cully was the chair of the tennis tournament last year." The lady described the house, and also the other woman. She had been standing next to Dad, acting as if our house was her house.

I wasn't ever formally introduced to the other woman. She just appeared, now with a name. Toni.

My parents divorced my senior year of college. The divorce was final in early June. He married the other woman on June 9. I graduated from UCLA on June 16. Dad skipped my college graduation, because Toni insisted on an immediate Hawaii honeymoon. I don't blame her. My graduation was going to be a family moment shortly after the family had been dismantled.

But of course I had to go to Dad's wedding. By then, they had moved to Phoenix, Arizona. It was never clear when they bought their new house. But it didn't matter. They had, and this wedding was on. My dad had invited his mother—whom we all called Mama Helen—to fly in from Omaha, but he had neglected to tell her the reason why. He couldn't tell her he was getting remarried, because, well, he hadn't told Mama Helen he'd gotten divorced.

It was Mama Helen's first flight, and she brought hard-boiled eggs and chicken packed in little baggies. She smelled up the plane, and since she was hard of hearing, she also spent the whole flight yelling.

Phoenix in June was *hell* degrees. When we arrived at Dad and Toni's house, we came upon a crew of aunts and girl cousins making homemade wedding souvenirs. Before she had time to figure out what was going on, someone rushed over and took Mama Helen out dress shopping "for an occasion."

My sisters and I joined our aunts at the table. Half of them had only just found out about the wedding themselves. Somebody looked up from the tchotchkes we were making and asked, "Did anybody tell Mama Helen?"

My father was called in.

"Did you tell Mama Helen you're getting married?" an aunt asked.

"I'm gonna tell her," he said.

"Does she know you're divorced?" said someone else.

"I'm gonna tell her. I'm gonna tell her."

The place went up in guffaws. "Oh, shit!" said a cousin, as the rest did impressions of my dad's frightened face.

When he finally got the nerve to tell his mother, shortly before the ceremony, Mama Helen's solidarity with my mom was like Sister Souljah. It was fascinating because, mind you, this woman was never a fan of my mother's. She called her "piss-colored" for the bulk of the marriage. But this whole deal didn't sit right with her. Not at all.

She decided to speak her mind at the church. My soon-to-be stepmother had a family member who was the pastor. He went on and on about this blessed union. That's when Mama Helen piped up from the front pew in her deaf-lady voice.

"She's a whore," she said to no one in particular, meaning the entire church. "Home-wrecker."

NOW, OUR BOYS CALL TONI NANA, AND SHE IS A LOVELY GRANDMOTHER. She and my dad still take their trips to Hawaii. People move on.

After the divorce, Mom left Pleasanton to move back to

Omaha. She was ready to start over. Instead of an easy retirement, she chose to help a relative who had a problem with drugs. This relative repeatedly got pregnant, and one by one, these babies came to live with my mother shortly after their births. This retirement-age woman adopted these children, now aged nine, eight, and six. Two beautiful girls and the youngest, a boy. My mother refused to let them be separated from each other.

She busts her ass to keep up with these kids. She has discovered emojis, this seventy-year-old woman, and she'll send me a wineglass with an exclamation point. She is also queen of the wink-and-tongue-out face.

I see you, Mom. I see what you are doing for these kids, and how you keep them together. I give you respect, because nobody is going to give you praise for doing what black women have done forever, raising kids who are not their own.

Nowadays, I catch myself starting conversations the way she used to. I think back to when we Union girls confronted her about this need to connect with strangers. It was just that she is a decent human being with a genuine curiosity about other human beings. She already knew what made my father tick, and the people of Pleasanton for that matter. They held no surprise.

"There are so many more people than you realize," she told us girls, "people who look up to the same sun and the moon and the stars. It's your birthright to explore this world."

It's only as small as you make it.

six

WHO HATES YOU MOST?

The cast of *Being Mary Jane* was holed up in a conference room while the crew investigated a gas leak on our Atlanta soundstage. Eventually we each reached the end of memes and Snapchat filters on our phones, so to kill time we started trading stories.

"Okay, who in your life has hated you the most?" someone asked.

People talked about a costar they'd gotten fired, an ex they brazenly cheated on. Amateur hour. Basic stuff. I knew I had the winner: a girl from high school named Queeshaun.

Queeshaun was best friends with Angela Washington, who was dating Jason Kidd when I met him. This was my junior year of high school, while I was technically dating Tyrone Reed, a stoner rebel from a nearby town. Tyrone had gotten his arm broken by the police, so obviously his cast had FUCK THE POLICE written on it in huge block letters. He would lean the cast out of his convertible VW bug when he drove around town. So rebellious.

Jason Kidd was the best high school player in the country, six foot four as a junior, and already famous among sports fans and college recruiters alike. His high school, St. Joseph's, could seat eight hundred in their gym. With Jason on the team, they were forced to move their games to a venue that seated five thousand, and people still got turned away.

I was in a Saturday afternoon girls' basketball tournament, and I stayed to watch the guys play. I was performing a bit, throwing out tips to the players, even Jason. It worked. Jason sat at the end of the bench, a towel around his neck. He knew everyone in that place was watching him, but he suddenly lifted his eyes to look right at me. It wasn't eye sex, just "I see you."

At half time, I went to the bathroom and there was Angela. I knew her from playing ball, because she was a star player for Livermore High. Our teams often competed against each other. Standing at the sinks, we talked about the game.

"That Jason is amazing," I said.

"Yeah," she said, "he is."

She walked out and went right over to Jason and I realized, Oh, she is totally his girlfriend. There went that idea.

At the end of the game, she left with Jason's parents, and he went over to the team bus. He lingered behind so I could catch up, and when I did, he asked for my number. We then proceeded to talk all hours for the rest of the weekend, and made a pact that on Monday I would break up with Tyrone and he would break up with Angela. We did so, with a generous round of "It's not you, it's me" for everyone.

I got right into being Jason's girlfriend and I wanted *everyone* to know it. I would go to my beloved Kim's Nails in Oakland, getting the letters of his name spelled out with a heart on my nails. J-A-S-O-N-K-I-D-D-♥. Don't judge me. I felt like a boss bitch.

The Friday before Christmas break, my school had a pep rally during lunchtime. My girlfriend Paige was a cheerleader, so I was right there, sitting with friends on a lunch table right at the front watching them perform. Fantasy Direct, a group of high-school-age DJs, was running the music. They were black and Latino, and from neighboring towns. But one, Hector, lived across the street from me.

Suddenly, this big black girl walked in with a determined stomp in her step. She had dookie braids, a pink ribbon woven into each one. She immediately stuck out to me, of course, because you know there were no other black girls around. Way across the room, I saw her go up to Hector, who then pointed in my direction. I looked behind me, thinking, Who could she possibly be looking for?

Then she started stalking through the crowd, about four or five people deep, around my lunch table. As she got closer, she lunged through a wall of people to get to me. But I still didn't understand that I was the target.

This girl is just really angry, I thought. Somebody is going to get their ass kicked. Meanwhile, the white people were practically clearing a path for her, just assuming that the black girl was there for the other black girl.

"I'm gonna whoop yo' ass, bitch!" she yelled at the top of her lungs, pointing right at me. "I'm gonna whoop yo' ass!"

I swear, I looked around like, "This couldn't possibly be about me." Eventually, the school security dragged her off school grounds by the shoulders. "I'm gonna get you, Nickie Union!" she yelled as they pulled her out the door. "I'm gonna come back after school and kick your ass!"

I was shaking as if I'd had a near-death experience. I had no idea who in the world this bitch was, and now all these white girls were staring at me.

"Oh my God," went the chorus. "Oh my God, are you okay? That was, like, so terrifying."

So I marched over to Hector and asked him why he sent her over to me.

"Oh, Queeshaun?" he said. "You don't know her?" He acted with total innocence. "She asked where you were. We thought you invited her."

"Hector, you know who comes to my house," I said. "And not a one looks like this bitch. Thanks a lot."

I immediately went to a pay phone and called my big sister Kelly. "COME GET ME NOW," I demanded, and I sat in the parking lot for the half hour it took for her to drive from San Jose State, where she was going to school. When I saw her, I stood up, waving like some castaway flagging down a helicopter.

"Where the hell is she?" she said, flying out of the car and darting her eyes around sniper style.

"She left," I said. "But she'll be back."

"We're gonna wait for her."

"Uh, no!" I started screaming. "Take me home!" I was not giving this girl a chance to come back and kill me.

"Nickie, you have to face her," she said. "Otherwise you're a coward."

"You stay, then," I said, getting into the car and locking the door. I waved. "Tell me how it goes!"

When my mom got home I kept talking about how I was

traumatized by "the day's events." I practically needed a fainting couch after what I had been through. But my teen/girlfriend priorities kicked in, and I asked my mom to take me to the mall because I still needed to get a Christmas gift for Jason.

We went to a Structure and I picked out the brighter of two Cosby-esque sweaters. I was smug as hell, having turned the day around. As we were getting ready to leave, I half-heartedly hummed along to the mall Muzak's "Jingle Bells." My mom and I went down the main escalator and I decided that crazy Queeshaun chick had the whole Christmas break to figure out she had me mixed up with another girl.

Midway down, my self-satisfied haze cracked. I saw my nightmare come to life in the form of Queeshaun standing at the bottom of the escalator, talking to, of all people, my freshly minted ex-boyfriend Tyrone, with his FUCK THE POLICE cast. They both looked up, and I immediately began trying to run up the down escalator.

"Nickie," my mom yelled, grabbing me by the back of my coat to stop me.

"Mom, that's her," I yelled. "That's her."

She turned and stared at Queeshaun, who couldn't believe her luck.

"I can't believe," Mom said, "you are scared of a girl wearing a bullet bra."

I had no idea what Queeshaun's bra had to do with me, since I was going to die at the bottom of that escalator. "I'm gonna whip yo' fuckin' ass for Angela," Queeshaun yelled, as we slowly moved toward her. "I don't care if your mama's here. I'mma whip yo' mama's ass, too."

As we reached bottom, Tyrone tried to drag Queeshaun away with his one good arm. I took the opportunity to run past them, but my mom stayed behind and got right in Queeshaun's face. Once Queeshaun said "I'll fight your mama," my mother—who is absolutely not this person—started nodding like Clair Huxtable about to school Theo, right there in front of Mrs. Field's Cookies. Mom wasn't about to fight this girl, though Queeshaun certainly would have come to blows with my mother. As Tyrone held Queeshaun back, my mother stood as tall and straight as can be. She was trying to show me the importance of standing your ground. Meanwhile, I was halfway down to McDonald's, yelling back, "Just come on!"

Finally, Mom relented and followed me. The whole car ride home I was shaking, but my mom had no sympathy whatsoever.

"That girl," she said. "She's got that fool bullet bra on. I can't believe you would be afraid of a girl like that."

"Mom. She came up to my school to kill me and she just tried again. Of course I'm scared."

"You should never be afraid of anyone. Certainly not the likes of her."

By the time we got home from the mall, Queeshaun had left a string of messages on our answering machine. This was one of those old-school answering machines, and my dad walked in to hear Queeshaun's threats.

"We'll just call her parents," he said. He then made a big deal of looking her family up in the phone book and calling her mother.

Satan's mom was not impressed.

"What are you gonna do? They're kids," she said. "Let our daughters handle it."

He hung up and right away, Queeshaun started burning up our phone. Cully Union told her to stop, and when she wouldn't, we just let her run out the answering machine tape. "Your monkey-ass dad is a snitch, bitch," she said. "I'm gonna kick his ass, too."

Dad being Dad, he decided to bring the whole answering machine to the police station. He played the tape for the all-white Pleasanton PD, and at first they were concerned. Then, as Queeshaun's insults and craziness took on the feel of a stereotypical crazy black woman comedy sketch, they couldn't stifle their laughter.

"Yo' monkey-ass daddy is a motherfucking punk nigger snitch" put them over the edge.

"Wait," a blond cop finally said, trying not to smile. "You don't even know her?"

"No," I said. "I swear."

"Why would she do this?"

"Apparently I hurt her feelings, because I started dating her best friend's boyfriend. Excuse me, ex-boyfriend."

That did it. The whole station erupted into guffaws.

"Look," said the blond guy. "This is not enough for us to go on. If she physically touches you, call us."

If she physically touched me, I knew I'd be dead. I took a break from imagining my funeral, lavish with tears, and called Jason to ask him about Queeshaun. He told me Queeshaun was rich and had a huge house. That came as a shock. It made no sense that someone rich would have dookie braids and want to kill me. One or the other I guess I could have comprehended, but both were overkill. The irony is that my initial assessment of her was exactly that of my white peers: If she has dookie braids, she must be poor. If she is a big black girl, she must be angry. Although in this case, this bitch really did want to kill me.

Jason thought it was funny that she was acting so crazy. "She's harmless," he said.

"Say that at my funeral," I told him. "This bitch is nuts."

Jason and I were still dating right into league basketball season. My team was set to play Angela's twice, and of course the first game was on her home turf of Livermore High. Angela stared at me on the court, and Queeshaun looked like she could barely contain herself in the stands, where she was sitting not so far from my "monkey-ass dad." I had begged Jason to come, but he couldn't because he also had a game. My sister was supposed to get off early from her job at the Limited so she could be there to protect me, but no such luck. My whole team was terrified, because everyone and her white mother had heard about Queeshaun.

I was a mess the whole game, unable to function as my hands shook in the layup line. Then I airballed so bad that my coach benched me. We lost, of course, and my teammates and I lingered inside as our coach went to bring the bus. Queeshaun paced back and forth, whispering to Angela. We knew that as soon as we left the gym, Queeshaun would follow us out and go in for the kill.

The stalling tactic was becoming embarrassing when suddenly the gym doors burst open. In walked my sister Kelly, in full Foxy-Brown-bent-on-vengeance mode. My hero, she had sped over straight from work, still in her black Limited blazer with the huge shoulder pads. I'd always loved my brilliant, take-charge sister, but never more than in that moment.

"Queeshaun?" she yelled. "You here?"

"Yep," Queeshaun said, stepping right up to Kelly.

"You so much as touch my sister, I will kill you."

And that did it. Queeshaun lunged forward. A couple of girls pulled her back. My sister was ride or die. She came over to me and threw her arm around my shoulder. "If you touch my sister," she said to all of Livermore, "I will kick every single one of your asses."

"That's right," I said, suddenly bold with my bodyguard beside me. "What she said."

She took me home. In the car, I did impressions of her Action Jackson performance. "I will spit on your grave, Queeshaun!"

The next time I played against Angela was completely a different story. Jason was there. Even better, Queeshaun wasn't. That let me talk trash straight to Angela, who was having her worst game of the season just as I had my best. I was so pleased with myself.

Jason and I were not at our best point, however. Instead of getting his full name across my nails, I was getting a subtle J and K painted. It was the nineties version of "It's complicated."

That spring I was at Kim's Nails with friends one afternoon, and just as the nail tech started in on the K, in walked Queeshaun. Did this bitch have a homing device on my freaking car? Her eyes snapped open from the surprise of seeing me, then narrowed with fury as she saw the J-K.

"Hold still," said the tech, as my hand started to shake.

"I told you the next time I saw you I was going to kick yo' ass, bitch!" My K not even finished, my friends threw down money and hustled me out the back door. It felt like I'd been in a stickup.

That seemed like the end. Cut to: the last day of junior year, and four of us were celebrating by sitting in Paige's car and oh-so-glamorously drinking Purple Passion in the parking lot of a strip mall. Lucy was in the front with Paige and I sat in the backseat with another friend, Sook, our doors open as we listened to the radio.

The song of the summer, Mariah's "Vision of Love," came on, and Paige turned it up *loud,* probably to drown us all out as we sang along. Just as I was pretending to hit that Mariah note, this meaty hand reached in and grabbed me by the arm, trying to drag me out of the car.

It was goddamned Queeshaun.

"I'm gonna kick your ass, bitch!" she screamed.

"What the fuck is wrong with you?" I yelled, as Sook held tight to my legs.

Paige pressed the gas, driving off with half of my body out the door. She did circles in the parking lot, swerving to try to shake Queeshaun as Mariah continued to belt. Sook managed to pull me in bit by bit, just like in the movies. It was kill or be killed. I tried to slam the car door on Queeshaun as Paige hit the gas to get the hell out of that parking lot.

Queeshaun started to run, that's how desperate she was to kick my ass! Finally, she tripped, let go, and hit the pavement. Hard.

"OH MY GOD," we said in one collective teen scream. Paige stopped the car.

"Is she dead?" I said.

Queeshaun instantly leapt up, and we all screamed. Again. First she moved toward us, then doubled back to get in her car. The bitch was *giving chase*. What was this zombie bitch?

We stopped at a light and she caught up to us, bumper to bumper. Paige pressed the gas, running the red to get away. Queeshaun stayed right on us. We went into the Meadows development, hoping to lose her in the cul-de-sacs. Paige even killed her lights and gunned it, relying on her knowledge of the twists and turns of suburban subdivisions. We finally shook her, and we saw a house party. We decided it was safer to hide out there.

We didn't mention Queeshaun to a single soul. On the one hand, we did kind of almost kill her and wanted deniability. On the other, she was like Beetlejuice—just saying her name could summon her.

When we left the party an hour later, there she was, sitting in her car, waiting for us. She'd spotted Paige's car. Of course she had. Now I had to choose between the social suicide of running back into the house and having Queeshaun follow me to beat me up in a Meadows party, or take my chances with the girls. It was that same fear of being associated with someone who looked like Queeshaun. I somehow got a pass, but I couldn't bring an agitated scary black girl to a party, because then I would be the scary black girl, too. Also, fighting was just unheard of in polite upper-middle-class suburban planned communities. It was more about emotional warfare.

"Get to the car," I whispered to Paige.

I stood by the door to the house party as the girls ran to the car.

"Come on, bitch," I said.

Queeshaun got out of her car and slammed the door. For a second, we stood frozen facing each other. Just as she started her charge onto the lawn, I cut left, fast, racing to Paige's car like I was doing the one-hundred-meter for the gold. By the time Queeshaun realized she'd been tricked and ran to get back in her car, we were tearing down the road.

We drove around Pleasanton all night. Each of us refused to go to our houses, afraid that Queeshaun would be lying in wait. Paige eventually parked at Foothill High, and we watched the sun begin to rise to Roxette's "It Must Have Been Love."

"Man," Sook said, as if she had been thinking one single thought through the whole song. "That Queeshaun really hates you."

Paige reenacted Queeshaun's rise up from the ground. "That is some Freddy Krueger–level crazy," she said to a mad chorus of laughter.

A few years later I met Freddy Washington, who is Angela's little brother, at UCLA. I asked Freddy if Angela still blamed me for Jason Kidd breaking up with her.

"No," he said. "Angela doesn't care."

"Oh, good," I said, relieved.

"But Queeshaun?" Freddy added with a sinister chuckle. "That crazy bitch still talks about you."

I flashed to her in a room with photos of me all over a wall. "Soon, Nickie Union," she said. "Soon."

MY *BEING MARY JANE* CASTMATES AGREED I WON THE CONTEST.

"Whatever happened to that girl?" my costar Lisa Vidal asked.

"No idea." Everyone grabbed his or her phone again, in a race to find Queeshaun. A particularly savvy Facebooker found a woman by her name. He held up his screen.

There she was. My high school nightmare, still looking like she would kick my ass in a second. She was presenting an office look, and I imagined all the coworkers she terrorized. From my reaction, everyone could tell it was her.

Lisa grabbed the phone to get a better look and screamed. "She's living in Atlanta!"

"Oh my God, she followed me here," I said, only half kidding.

The door to the conference room swung open and every single one of us seasoned professionals *jumped*. We all expected to see Queeshaun standing there, yelling her trusty catchphrase: "I told you the next time I see you I'mma kick yo' ass!"

"We're all clear, guys," said the production assistant, eyeing us with suspicion.

We were safe. For now.

seven

CODE 261

I worked there with all my friends that summer after freshman year of college. It was an easy job. You didn't have to help *anyone,* that's the beauty of Payless shoe stores. The customers help themselves and you just have to ring them up. So you can kind of fuck around all day and get paid.

It was near the end of July, the time of the big Garth Brooks concert. Everyone had tickets and they needed someone to cover. It was assumed that I didn't like Garth. Black girls don't want to see country music. But I would have loved to see Garth. *No Fences* was one of my favorite albums, and I knew every single word to "Friends in Low Places." But of course, Nickie can work that night. The black girl and the Goth girl—they'll cover.

I was nineteen.

Someone was hitting Payless stores that summer, but we didn't know a thing. He was a former employee, black. The management and police had positively identified him because he robbed the same store where he used to work. They had a description, even his driver's license information. Then he hit a second store. Mind you, Payless would send you a storewide alert to change the price of a shoe or tell you how to display new sandals. They had the ability to warn us about this guy, tell us to be on the lookout for this former employee. They had pictures and a driver's license. And since our store was in a predominantly white community, if a black guy walked in, we would pick up on him right away. And yet, we weren't told a thing. Not a peep about the robberies.

Our store had even been hit before, but by someone else. Goth Girl had been there then, but no one got hurt. Every other Payless store that had ever been robbed now had security measures, like cameras and panic buttons. Not ours. And we were right by the freeway, such an easy mark.

So a black man walks into a Payless just before closing . . .

When he first walked in, I was in the back of the store straightening up a display of fake Timberlands in the men's department. When it was two to the store, one person worked the register, one worked the floor. He came up behind me and asked me about the boots. I don't remember what he asked, because I took one look at him and I immediately wanted to run. I didn't. I ignored my instincts. Part of that was the racial component of where I lived. I was very aware of how my coworkers and the people in the community viewed black people. So my instincts said, "Run. Run. This is a bad situation." But my racial solidarity and my "good home training" as a "polite" woman said, "Stay put. Don't feed a stereotype. Don't be rude."

He went back to the front and I started vacuuming. This was at eight forty-five. We weren't supposed to vacuum until the store actually closed at nine, but this was a trick staffers did to tell customers that it was closing time, get the fuck out.

The vacuum was so loud, and I heard Goth Girl scream to me to come to the register. Something in her voice told me to run. Again, I didn't. I overruled my instincts and walked to the front, where he was holding a gun on her. He motioned to me with the gun to get behind the register. As Goth Girl gave him the money, he was incredulous that there was only a couple of hundred. As a former employee, he knew there should be more.

"I already did the drop," she said, referring to walking the pouch of money to the nearby bank. It was another way we cut closing corners to clock out early. She sounded more annoyed than frightened. She had been there during the previous robbery and wasn't hurt. And being an entitled young person, she had the luxury of being angry.

"Go in the back," he said when he had emptied the cash into his bag.

Goth was in front of me, and the gun was in my back as he marched us to the storeroom. The gun was in *my* back, and she was still cursing him out, kicking boxes all the way in.

"This is such bullshit," she said as he closed the storeroom door behind us. "I can't believe this is happening."

"Take off your clothes."

Goth was still pissed. "I'm not taking my clothes off."

Mind you, I was naked in a second. It never even occurred to me to say no.

We'll be naked and dead when they find us, I thought.

And then he told us to both get in the bathroom.

Okay, I thought, maybe he'll just put us in the bathroom. Maybe he's doing this to buy time so he can leave.

So we crammed into the tiny little bathroom. And then, seconds later, he ordered me out.

He threw me to the ground and was suddenly on me, spreading my legs as he kept the gun on my head.

As he raped me, I began to hover over myself. I could see the whole room. I looked at that poor crying girl as she was being raped and thought, Things like this happen to bad people. Things like this don't happen to people like me. My psyche, my body, my soul, simply could not take it. Though people say things like "I saw my whole life flash before my eyes," I can tell you that this didn't happen to me. I didn't see my life. I was just very much present at the scene, watching this man rape me with a gun to my head.

He turned me over to go for it doggy style. He put the gun down, placing it right next to me. I wasn't looking at him, obviously, but staring at his gun.

"Can you hand me the gun?"

He said it just like that, as he ripped into me. He said it so very casually. "Can you hand me the gun?" It wasn't even "Gimme the gun." It wasn't forceful or gruff. It was like he was asking for the salt.

"Can you hand me the gun?"

And in that moment, when he asked me to give him the gun, the me that was hovering above and the me getting raped became *one.* I was back in my body, and I grabbed that motherfucking gun.

I moved forward, turned, and landed on my back. And I shot at him.

I can go right back to that moment now. The sound of the gunshot reverberating in my ears, every muscle in my hurting body tensed, the smell of gunpowder filling the air.

And the realization that I missed. And that I was probably going to die very soon.

He jumped on me, trying to yank the gun out of my fist. He bashed my face as he turned the gun toward me with his other hand.

My finger was wedged between the trigger and the base of the gun. It felt like he was going to rip my finger off, but I wouldn't let go. I flashed on scenes from movies, so I kept trying to pull the trigger seven times. I just thought that if I clicked it seven times, I would save myself. I was trying to turn the gun away from my face *and* holding on to it *and* trying to pull the trigger all at the same time.

I kept screaming for Goth to come out and help me. She didn't come out.

Finally, he ripped the gun out of my hand. He pointed the barrel at my head as he stood over me.

"Now I'm gonna have to kill you, bitch."

I looked down, begging, my face a mess of blood and tears. I clutched a gold-plated chain necklace my boyfriend Alex had given me.

"You can have this," I sputtered. "Take it. It's worth more than the money you got. Take it."

He had already taken everything else from me. This necklace was all I had to offer for my life.

He didn't take the necklace. I didn't dare look at him. And as quickly as it all happened, he was calm. And again, he said, very casually.

"How do I get out of here?"

I pointed to the back exit, whimpering, snorting tears and the thick blood back into my nose.

He went out and I was left alone. I never saw him again.

I called for Goth. I didn't ask why she hadn't come out. I knew why. In those moments, you do what you need to do to stay alive, I guess. Self-preservation is a motherfucker.

I DON'T REMEMBER WHICH ONE OF US CALLED 911, BUT THE POLICE GOT there fast. I am grateful I was raped in an affluent neighborhood with an underworked police department. And an underutilized rape crisis center. And overly trained doctors and nurses and medical personnel. The fact that one can be grateful for such things is goddamn ridiculous.

Two cops arrived initially, and then there were more. Many more. If they had been writing a manual for police officers and medical personnel on how to handle a rape case with care and compassion, I would have been the perfect test case on procedure. They were wonderful. And I know this now because I have spent time lobbying Congress and state legislatures about the treatment of rape victims. I've seen the worst-case scenarios, and they are devastating. Now, I can appreciate the care with which I was handled. Now, I know it rarely happens that way. And it *really* rarely happens that way for black women. I am grateful I had the experience I did, wrapped up in the worst experience of my life. Now.

Then, I was hysterical. I'm not a hysterical person. I'm not even a weepy person. And I was hysterical. I looked up, and suddenly my dad and my older sister, Kelly, were just there at the store. Later, I would find out they were running errands and saw the police cars lined up outside the Payless where I worked. But in that moment, it just seemed surreal to suddenly have them there.

"Calm down," my dad kept saying, over and over again, as he touched my shoulder. I couldn't speak to tell him what happened and I couldn't imagine telling him anyway.

The cops were radioing dispatch and other officers using police codes, a jumble of numbers wrapping around my head. None of them meant anything.

But Kelly was majoring in criminal justice. And I saw her face when she recognized the police code for rape: 261.

She whispered in Dad's ear. And the way he looked at me after, oh my God, is still a nightmare. I sued Payless for negligence, but I wanted to sue them for my dad looking at me like that. I HATED THAT. To this day, I HATE IT.

The look was: Damaged. Victim. Guilt. Fear. Like, I was my dad's prize. He didn't acknowledge it in words, but I was his favorite because I was the most like him. As far as he was concerned, I followed the rules. I was the kid you bragged about. I got great grades. Was the perfect athlete. Blah blah blah. And in that moment I was *damaged.* It was as if someone had broken his favorite toy.

I was taken to the hospital. After having my dad see me in that moment, my boyfriend Alex came to the hospital. And he too was destroyed. We'd been together about a year. His family was Greek and Mexican, and they were completely opposed to us being together. They called him a nigger lover.

"But you're an interracial couple!" he would answer.

"Why do you have to go to the extreme?" was the response.

Yet in the moment of Alex finding out I'd been raped and his parents having to deal with their child being crushed, they finally realized that our thing was real. I was, to put it mildly, very resentful that it took my being raped for them to not have a problem with interracial dating. But anyway.

My mom arrived, quiet and scared. I flashed to the advice my mom had given my older sister and me for how to handle anyone who wanted to mug us or worse.

"You know what you do, right?"

We would say in unison with matching eye rolls: "What do we do, Mom?"

"You say 'Shit, shit bastard!' That's what you do."

Shit, shit bastard. She thought a woman spewing out a string of nonsense swears would shock an assailant into confused submission. To this day my sisters and I will just text those words to each other, or leave "Shit, shit bastard" on each other's voice mails.

She didn't know what to say to me. I'm sure she was shocked because it happened to the one daughter she didn't think she had to worry about. I had always been the strongest one, taking care of myself. They had never seen me show fear. You move your kids to this all-white community and force them to go to these all-white schools. You think you've priced yourself out of this shit. You've done all these things and then this happens.

A FEW DAYS LATER, THE GUY STRUCK AGAIN IN A NEIGHBORING CITY. YOU could see him on the security camera at Payless this time. He walked in, saw the camera, and walked right back out. But then I guess he was just amped up to keep this crime spree going and he walked into a Clothestime store. I knew the girl there. He'd become more brazen, bolder, and he hurt her even more than he hurt me. By then the manhunt was reaching fever pitch. Within the week, he turned himself in. Because they knew who he was, the cops had started watching his mother's house, and she got him to surrender.

My dad was the one who went to every arraignment. Every single court hearing. I remember Dad saying, "I want him to see me." He is one of those parents who can rule with a look. Discipline with a glare. And he really thought that the same glare that got us to stop jumping on the bed, or to eat our vegetables, was going to work on someone who'd raped women. But he was there. Glaring.

"*Now* I feel bad," my rapist would say. "Not when I was smashing her crying face or leaving her in a heap. Nope. But her father's glare. That did it. That's what made me see the evil I had done." Dad took it personally, so this wasn't about justice for me. It was a personal affront to him. It happened to me, but it was an affront to him.

To this day, my dad has the article from the newspaper about my rape in his wallet. Twenty-four years. He has never explained to me why he carries it around, but I know it's a reminder that someone dared to fuck with him. "How dare you even think you could do this to *me*?"

Because of that article, everybody knew. They didn't print my name, but there were very few black people my age in Pleasanton. And just in case, for the people who didn't know, Lisa Goodwin went to a party and to get sympathy for herself, told *my* story but made it about how it affected *her*.

I had to testify in front of a grand jury, but I didn't have to see him. The most traumatizing part was going into the courthouse and seeing other criminals. I could see them coming off the transport van in shackles. Coming face-to-face with criminals, being in the courthouse with rapists and murderers and child molesters, was, for somebody in the throes of post-traumatic stress, all too much. I got into the elevator and in two seconds, I literally sprinted back out. Wrong combination of people. I heard my mom apologize because I guess she probably thought it looked rude.

He took a plea deal of thirty-three years. So we never had to go to a *trial.* I hope he's still in jail. I haven't looked to see if he's out. I do know he is aware of who I've become. My father said they mentioned it in one of the parole proceedings. My dad goes to those, too.

I have seen enough episodes of *Oz* that I really believe in prison justice. I believe there are certain things that prisoners do very well. And their handling of rapists is one of them. So . . . I feel pretty solid about that. Whatever he's endured brings me joy. I hope it happens every day of his life. A few times a day. I'm perfectly okay with that.

People always ask, "Do you wish you'd had better aim?" I mean, obviously you pull the trigger of a gun to stop, maim, or kill. That was my goal in that split second. But I don't think I'm a killer. I don't think I could live with killing anyone, even in self-defense. I think I would be even more tortured by that.

The other question I get asked is "What were you wearing?" I got raped at work and people still want to know what role I played in what happened to me.

I HAD ALREADY TRANSFERRED FROM THE UNIVERSITY OF NEBRASKA AND was supposed to start UCLA in August. But I couldn't do the grand jury and be in Los Angeles, so I deferred and did a semester of my sophomore year at a junior college in Fremont. During that time, I opted to sue Payless for not providing a safe environment.

Timing became the most important thing in my life. I timed everything I did to try to reduce the space for something else to happen to me. If I could limit the time I was in, say, a restaurant, then that would narrow the likelihood of me being murdered if the restaurant was held up in a hostage situation. That's how my brain began to function.

There were times when I was studying in the library, and I lost track of time and let it get dark out. Then I had to get from the library to my car. I'd run to my car, jump in, slam the door, and slump into the seat in a heap of tears. I'd shake, my arm numb as if I were having a heart attack—and I had to sit and wait. My car at the time was a stick shift and I couldn't stop my foot from shaking to put my car in gear, so I had to just sit. But sitting meant a carjacking was possible.

I moved from the fear of one random act of violence to another, because I'd seen the devil up close. Once you've been the victim of a violent crime and you have seen evil in action, you know the devil lives and breathes in people all day, every day.

The first therapist I saw was a bust. I saw him about two weeks after I was raped. He very quickly diagnosed me with post-traumatic stress disorder and insisted on trying to hypnotize me. A person who has just been raped isn't into that mind control shit, I assure you. He tried several times, and I would scrunch my face, pretending, but in my mind I'd be organizing my closet. I was also struck that he thought I was so Humpty Dumpty broken that he couldn't even talk to my conscious self. It's like he was looking past me to say, "Let me talk to your manager. I need to see someone who's really in charge here."

One of the first weeks of classes at UCLA, I saw an ad in the *Daily Bruin* for mental health services.

I visited the clinic and realized that the UCLA Rape Crisis Center was a part of mental health services. And through the Rape Crisis Center, there was group therapy. And you could meet other rape survivors. And so I got rid of Mr. Hypnotism and started seeing a therapist through UCLA.

In group, I was the only stranger rape. The rest of the students had been raped by acquaintances or family members. Some studies have estimated that 90 percent of rapes perpetrated against college-age women are acquaintance rapes. You want to know something weird? I felt grateful that my rapist was a stranger. It felt like a luxury not knowing the person. Because there was no gray area. There was no question of "Who are they going to believe, him or me?"

I was also the only one in the group who'd gone through the criminal justice system. Some of these women still had classes with these guys. One woman, I think she was an engineering student, was raped by her lab partner. But she had to go right back. I don't remember if she was the one who ended up dropping out. I know she wanted to, because the engineering department was so small and she felt trapped.

Group therapy was the only place I could feel "not crazy." I was around other young people with the same stresses I have, the same fears and triggers. You know that feeling you get when somebody first rubs your feet? It's like a jolt through your whole body, then an instant exhale.

Each time we met, I exhaled. Because when you've been raped, you really feel like you're on an island. Rape is the most underreported crime there is. And it's shrouded in secrecy and shame. You think no one will be able to relate to you because of what you've been through. Then to be in this room, where *everyone* could relate, changed everything. *Wow, that girl is getting straight As. That girl got a great internship. This girl is engaged.* It gave me the calm I so desperately needed. I saw the possibility of hope.

My therapist was lovely. "Let's talk," she said to me the first time we met. "Just talk." Unlike my previous therapist, she didn't treat me as someone irrevocably broken. She gave me glue, some Band-Aids, and Bactine, and said, "You've got this."

At UCLA, my life was like that cartoon where someone is walking along and magically a new plank is placed before them with each new step. It felt like there was nothing beneath me, but then each visit, each story, each memory was like another plank. I had no idea where those planks were taking me, but I was hoping that healing was on the other side. Being able to function was on the other side. Not having to literally run in panic all the time was on the other side.

And then, before I got to the other side, I went and got famous.

THERE'S A VISE AROUND MY CHEST AND MY ARMS ARE NUMB. IF I HAD TO swim for my life, I would die right now. It's like a slow-moving heart attack. Those dreams where something is happening but you can't move—that's my life.

And this is twenty-four years later.

I am in the car outside Target. I am talking myself into going in. I have a list clutched in my hand, because it's a sort of security blanket of order. I have to be as efficient as possible, get in and get out. And it's also something to stare at if I am being stared at. In my head I rehearse the walk to the door, and I gauge how well I did choosing one of the times that the store is less crowded. I won't feel safe, not even when I am back in my car. I will feel only safe when I am home. When every door is locked and checked.

After I was raped, in 1992, I didn't leave my house for a whole year unless I had to go to court or to therapy. I simply did not leave. That spiraled into me not going anywhere that I could be robbed. Anyplace where there was money exchanged, I simply avoided. The other day I was telling my husband that I couldn't remember the last time that I actually went into a bank. The idea of being in there while it was robbed—that shallow-breathing-inducing fear of "I could be robbed right now"—is too much for me. Anytime I go to a restaurant with someone, I joke, "Sorry, the Malcolm X in me can't sit with my back to the door." But I can't. I cannot enjoy a meal if my back is to the door.

Twenty-four years.

That feeling of surveillance, of being hunted, never goes away. Fear influences everything I do. I saw the devil up close, remember. And I see now how naïve I was. Of course I can never truly have peace again. That idea is fiction. You can figure out how to move through the world, but the idea of peace? In your soul? It doesn't exist.

I often get asked if my fears have decreased as I move further from the rape. No. It's more about me moving from becoming a rape victim to a rape survivor. I am selective about who I allow into my life. I can spot people who make me feel anxious or fearful, and they are not welcome.

But with the accessibility of our culture, I can't keep boundaries. It could be the guy who grabs me, yelling, "YOU KNOW YOU WANT TO GET THIS PICTURE!" People will grab me as I'm walking through a crowd. They may turn it into a joke, but they are also not taking no for an answer. No one understands how much female celebrities are physically touched and grabbed and shoved and fondled. We all talk about it. I can't tell you how many times people—men and women—feel your body. "Oh, you're just a little bitty thing," I hear, with someone squeezing my thigh. Men take pictures and get you under the armpit so they can feel the side of your boob. But we're supposed to just take it.

I was talking to someone about this recently. "You have a lot of rape energy around you," he said. "Something happening to you that you had no power to stop. And it keeps happening."

The first time I said no, my ex-husband Chris and I were on a casino floor in Vegas. We were having a huge argument and I was crying. I stared down at the incredibly tacky carpet of giant red and green flowers surrounded by gilded latticework. I followed the loop of the lace over and over with my eyes, hoping to disappear into the rug. But I felt something. Even before I heard the yell, I sensed I was in someone's sights.

"Bring it on!"

It was a cheerleading squad first marching, then running toward me. They were in full regalia, head to toe, clearly in town for a cheerleading competition.

"It's already been brought!" they yelled.

I was still sobbing as they surrounded us. "I am so sorry," I said, practically heaving. "It's not a good time, girls."

They looked so disappointed, curling their lips to smile at me, willing my ugly cry away.

When they finally walked away, I felt a wave of panic that I'd let these people down. I wanted to call them back. "I can do this!" I wanted to yell. "I can be what you need!" I still think about that moment.

I can remember each time I said no, because I have panic attacks about backlash. When my husband Dwyane and I are together, we've got double the attention. Don't get me wrong—I'm incredibly grateful to represent something so very positive to a group of people, but the flipside is that each interaction is anxiety producing for me and an opportunity for me to disappoint yet again. I have such a fear of not fulfilling the ever-changing wants and needs and expectations of strangers that I become terrified of what should be basic encounters. Going into a bar with friends, I'm like a rabbit that has wandered into a yard where a pack of wild dogs lives. One minute, I'm just hanging, chilling with all the other rabbits. Then something picks up my scent, and I've gotta flee.

When we're out with the boys we raise, Zaire, Dahveon, and Zion, we try to say, "Hey, guys, it's family time." Not so long ago, we were all at brunch in Miami and an entire family came over. Mind you, we were in the middle of a family discussion, and also just really enjoying being together. It was one of the very few times I was not completely on edge out in public, looking around, checking for the emergency exits.

Zaire, who was twelve at the time, took the lead and jokingly said, "Not a good time."

The mom looked at me. "Is this what you're allowing?"

"We're just trying to enjoy breakfast," I said in my sweetest actress voice.

She grabbed my arm. Like you would grab a kid who is about to fall in the pool. She used full force. She wanted my attention.

"That's a shame," she hissed.

This woman snatched me, right in front of my family. I try to teach the kids about boundaries and sticking up for yourself and not letting people show you disrespect, and then I am grabbed in front of them.

"*What* is a shame?" I asked. There was no answer.

It happened so fast. It was so shocking.

D intervened. *"Not now,"* he told the woman.

It is twenty-four years later. My instinct in so many situations when I feel threatened is to *run.* As fast as I can. But just as that night at Payless, my good home training keeps me frozen in fear.

And then, sometimes, we humans perceive each other.

I will be in the ladies' room, washing my hands next to another woman. She will take a few glances, which I notice, and as I'm readying myself to walk out the door, she'll say, "Me, too."

She doesn't have to tell me what she means. I nod. I have been doing rape advocacy and sharing my own story since the beginning of my career. We don't hug. We don't cry. She nods back at me. Just two women in a moment of mutual respect, acknowledging the truth and consequences of our experience. Feeling, in that moment, less alone on our respective islands.

eight

BLACK WOMAN BLUES

"You know, you are really pretty for a dark-skinned girl."

The woman placed her hand on mine as she said this. We had just met. This black lady had stopped me at the airport to say she enjoyed *Being Mary Jane*. She delivered her remark about beauty with a tone of assurance, yet surprise.

For years, whenever I heard this I would tighten my lips into an impassive smirk, tilt my head as if I didn't really understand what the person was saying, and move the conversation elsewhere. Or simply end it. I know, it sounds like I was just called pretty. I get that it can be confusing. The phrase is used in the black community as if a unicorn had just been spotted prancing across 125th Street. Through God all things are possible, and it's even possible that He sometimes makes dark-skinned women who aren't ugly. Somehow, some way, I escaped the curse of my melanin and Afrocentric features to become a credit to my skin tone. "We found one!"

An ex-friend I came up with in Hollywood used to say, "I just think it's great that you are so dark and still able to book jobs." She was the slightest shade lighter than me. I let it go until I simply let her go, but recently, I've grown tired of ignoring these remarks and what they mean about all darker-skinned women. Issues of colorism run so deep in the African American community, but more and more I see it spring up on social media as #teamlightskin versus #teamdarkskin. It's an age-old us-against-us oversimplification that boils down to the belief that the lighter your skin tone, the more valuable and worthy you are. The standard of beauty and intelligence that has historically been praised by the oppressor has been adopted by the oppressed.

This value system has become ingrained in us. As a teen, I became obsessed with the attention of boys, and equally fixated, if not more so, on the light-skinned girls who, I felt, would walk into a room and immediately snatch that attention away. I disliked them on sight.

My mother is light skinned, and she grew up having girls say to her face: "You think you're so much better than me." Mom and her sisters saw their light skin as a burden. They were called piss colored and listened to chants of "light, bright, and damn near white." My mother told me that she married a darker-skinned black man because she didn't want her kids to have "light-skin problems." I can imagine my grandmother's face when Mom brought home Cully Union.

My mother felt the burden, but I witnessed the privilege. Inheriting my father's skin, but growing up in proximity to my mother's lightness and to the lightness of my cousins, I saw how people across the whole color spectrum responded differently to them than they did to me. In my view, there was simply no comparison in our plights. It was impossible not to grow to resent that.

We darker girls should not be pitted against our lighter-skinned sisters, but our pain at being passed over also shouldn't be dismissed by people saying, "Love the skin you're in." You can love what you see in the mirror, but you can't self-esteem your way out of the way the world treats you. Not when we are made to feel so unloved and exiled to the other end of the beauty spectrum.

I e-mailed a young friend of mine telling her that I wanted to write about colorism. She replied immediately. "Sometimes it makes me feel crazy," she told me, "because when I bring up the issue it's met with confusion or disbelief." This gorgeous young woman blessed with darker skin had tried to self-esteem herself into fulfillment for years, but her experience with colorism left her feeling hopelessly alone. My friend had no problem getting a date, but finding amazing black men who truly love darker-skinned women proved to be a challenge. "The truth is, there are just certain men that are not and will never check for you," she says. "At least not seriously."

Perhaps more isolating, whenever she has raised the issue of colorism with friends or men, she is told that she is creating and encouraging division within the community. "People tell me I'm just imagining these feelings," she said; they think she's exaggerating the effects of colorism she experiences professionally and socially.

She's not. She is not imagining this shit, and she is not alone. For decades, sociologists like Margaret Hunter have collected real empirical evidence that we are color struck. Darker-skinned people face a subset of racial inequalities related to discipline at school, employment, and access to more affluent neighborhoods. In one study, Hunter found that a lighter-skinned woman earned, on average, twenty-six hundred dollars more a year than her darker sister. In her 2002 study of the color stratification of women, Hunter also presented real statistical evidence showing that light-skinned African American women had "a clear advantage in the marriage market and were more likely to marry high-status men than were darker-skinned women."

I have my own case study. My first husband was dark skinned, and I was the darkest-skinned woman he ever dated. Once he got a little success in football, he told me, "I wanted the best." What he considered the best, a sign that he had "made it," was dating light-skinned girls. It showed he had the ability to break through class and color barriers. He chose to marry me because I was famous and had money. For him, that trumped color.

"The number-one draft pick or the up-and-coming action hero will never choose me, because I'm dark skinned," my friend said. On the other hand, she has sometimes felt fetishized by men who briefly date her solely for the visual. "After Lupita got big, I noticed it was trendy to like me," she said. "On that note, white men *love* me. It's almost like a validation for them. 'Look at this black woman on my arm, natural hair, black skin, natural ass . . . See, I'm down!'

"It's hard to gauge who really likes me," she continued, "and who just wants to use me as an accessory. I've been told repeatedly that I'm not worthy, so when someone says that I *am,* it feels like a setup."

When black men are just honest with me, they admit that their vision of success most often does not include *expanding* on their blackness. "It's lightening up my gene pool," one guy boldly told me. "If I have a baby with you, we're gonna have a black-ass baby." When Serena Williams, whose fiancé is white, announced her pregnancy, a light-skinned black guy with twenty-one thousand followers announced on Twitter: "Can't blame her for needing a lil' milk in her coffee to offset those strong genes for generations to come."

That's some shit, and it hurts. We talked about the disconnect between the adoration so many black men shower on their mothers and grandmothers and their refusal to spend the rest of their lives with a woman who resembles their hue. "Why isn't the same type of woman good enough or even worth considering?" she asked me. "And do they even know they're doing this?"

There is another question I have to ask. Aren't these men also acutely aware of what it is to move through this world in the body of a dark brown boy? These men grow up seeing how people with lighter skin are respected and treated differently. Dark skin is weaponized and continually used against us day to day. What if it's not simply preference or acquiring a status symbol, but a learned tactic of survival?

I say this as someone who was certainly guilty of being color struck when I began dating. In my junior year of high school, I knew I was cute because I began pulling people that dark-skinned black girls were not supposed to pull. That was the barometer of my beauty: who and what I was winning in spite of my blackness. These boys were all top athletes, and I saw the admiration my dad had for me as I was dating them. My dad would go to their games and invite neighbors over to meet them. The more he bragged, the more validated I was that I was doing something right. "If I don't pull somebody that other people want and that crowds actually *cheer for* . . ." The stakes got higher and higher.

Eventually I didn't necessarily need to be the girlfriend. I just needed these guys to choose me in the moment, over someone else. That line of thinking can get you very sexually active very quickly. And it just kind of got away from me. You find yourself, a couple of Keystone Lights in, kissing some random guy in the bathroom of a house party. Some guy you don't know at all, who maybe isn't even your type, but just looked your way . . . and you needed that validation fix.

For the longest time, I wouldn't date anyone darker than me. It was so ingrained in me that I didn't see it as an active choice that I was friend-zoning anyone with more melanin than me. In my early twenties, someone finally did an intervention. I was having lunch with my older sister and one of her guy friends, Eric, at a soul food spot, of all places. I was wearing a T-shirt emblazoned with ERASE RACISM. I was making some point about power structures in relationships, feeling woke as fuck.

"Well, let's talk about how you're color struck," said Eric.

"Excuse me?" I said.

"I've known you since you were, what, twelve, thirteen?" he said. "The guys you've said you had crushes on and the guys that you dated, none of them are darker than you. A lot of them are a *lot* lighter than you. Have you thought about why that is?"

"Look," I said, "I actually don't think about that stuff. Love sees no color."

"Bullshit," he said. "To say 'love sees no color' is dumb as fuck. If that beautiful love of yours were kidnapped, you wouldn't go to the police and say, 'Help, a lovely soul was snatched off the street . . .'"

"No," I said, making a face in the hope that we'd just drop it.

"You'd give a thorough-ass description," he said. "Height, weight, scars, and you'd start with skin color and tone. You actually do see each other, quite clearly, and that's amazing."

I pretended to be really intent on my mac and cheese.

"Love sees everything," Eric said. "You're making a choice. And when you make that choice of putting yourself in a position to fall in love with a very specific person who looks nothing like yourself, that does actually say something about your choices."

So I got real. Right there, in my now ridiculous Erase Racism shirt, I opened up about my choices. I talked about feeling passed over for white and lighter-skinned girls and the rush I felt every time I got someone they were supposed to get. As I spoke, I realized it had so little to do with the actual guy. It wasn't my preference for light-skinned guys. It was all about their preference for me.

People underestimate the power of conversation. That lunch intervention gave me permission to like other people. If I could truly love my own skin, then I was not going to see darker skin as a threat to my worthiness and my value. Then it was come one, come all.

Shortly after, I met my cousin's former football teammate Marlin, whose nickname was literally Darkman. Marlin was midnight black, with a perfect smile and a gorgeous body. I met him at this massive sports bar called San Jose Live, and he had such enthusiasm about the music playing that with every new song he was like, "That's my jam!" He was a hard dancer, meaning that you'd feel like a rag doll keeping up, but he was sweet. We ended up dating for two years, until I met my first husband and broke up with him. My first husband was chocolate brown, beefy, and covered in tattoos. He didn't look like anyone I had dated, either.

When I got divorced and I went flying through my bucket list of dicks, they came in all shapes and sizes. This new approach was liberating. I felt open like a twenty-four-hour Walmart on freaking Black Friday.

Once I dated black men, I felt like I could breathe. Exhale and inhale deeply, without the anxiety of being examined by others to ensure that I was the "right kind of black" to even qualify to date interracially. When I dated nonblack men, there was always the *Get Out* fear of meeting their parents. My college boyfriend's parents were nice to my face but called him a nigger lover and accused him of screwing up his life dating a black girl. Now I no longer had to endure the constant evaluations of my character, looks, and accomplishments from his friends and from strangers witnessing a white man being publicly affectionate with me. It drove me crazy to watch them look at us, puzzling out the equation of why I would be worthy of his touch. I could breathe.

I think that might be the biggest reason so many people root for me and Dwyane. He chose an undeniably black woman. When you have struggled with low self-esteem, to have anyone root for you feels good. To have women rooting for you who have been in your shoes and felt the pain you felt, feels likes a thousand little angel wings beating around you.

OF COURSE COLORISM ISN'T JUST CONFINED TO BEING AFRICAN AMERIcan. Or even American. In 2011, I went to Vietnam to film the *Half the Sky* documentary with Nicholas Kristof, a Pulitzer Prize–winning columnist for the *New York Times*. We were there to delve into issues around education and young women, but when we landed, I immediately saw all these surgical masks. I wondered what I was walking into. Was there some kind of viral outbreak? If so, I was going to need one of those masks. It was also oppressively hot, yet people wore long-sleeved shirts with every inch of skin covered by fabric.

Oh, I thought, it might just be the usual, run-of-the-mill epidemic of colorism. I started asking questions, because I think it's important to have that conversation and examine our value systems. I noticed I wasn't getting a straight answer through the translator. People acted like they had no idea what I was talking about. When I finally met a blunt local teenager who could speak English, I jumped on the chance to ask about all the covering up.

"Oh," she said immediately, "nobody wants to get darker."

It was that simple. I could tell it immediately dawned on her that she'd just told a black person that nobody wants to get dark. So she switched to "they."

"They want their color to be just like him," she continued, pointing to a crew member traveling with me. "White."

"So what happens if you happen to get dark?" I asked.

"Like the people who work in the fields?" she asked. "They think it's ugly."

It smacked me right between the eyes. "They think it's ugly," I repeated, letting the phrase hang in the air.

"Yeah, but if it's vacation dark, it's more like a sign of wealth," she said. "If you're just *dark* dark, it's a sign that you're poor and you work in the sun doing manual labor. And no one wants to be associated with that."

I have now had these conversations with girls all over the world, from Asia to South America, Europe to Africa. When I am traveling, I see billboards on the streets with smiling light-skinned models promising the glory of brightening and lightening therapies. Take Fair & Lovely, an extremely profitable Unilever lightening cream that the company boasts has been transforming lives for the better since 1975. Sold in forty countries, this melanin suppressor is the best-selling "fairness cream" in the world. Seriously, Unilever says that *one in ten* women in the world use it. In India, the ads have changed with time from the original focus on getting a man—"if you want to be fair and noticed"—to becoming lighter in order to get a *job*. One career girl ends the commercial looking at her new face in the mirror. "Where have *you* been hiding?" she asks herself.

We're right here and we're hiding in plain sight.

"FOR A BLACK GIRL YOU SURE ARE PRETTY!"

This is the white cousin of "pretty for a dark-skinned girl." To fully understand colorism, we have to acknowledge the root. Just as dark-skinned girls are often only deemed deserving of praise *despite* their skin tone, black women as a whole are often considered beautiful despite their blackness.

I have heard this often, coming from left field at work or meeting someone new. One time that sticks out was when I heard it in the parking lot of my twentieth high school reunion in Pleasanton a few years back. The guy was drunk and so was I, since I'd grabbed vodka as soon as I walked in to dull the effects of standing out so much. I wasn't sure if it was my fame or my blackness that made everyone say, "Oh, there she is." I had forgotten that long before I was ever on-screen, I already was famous in Pleasanton. I was the black one.

We were in the parking lot, figuring out where to go for the second hang. It was not lost on me that I was with the same crew that went to all the bonfires. The guy said it out of nowhere as if he perceived me for the first time and had to qualify his regard with a caveat.

"Why do you say, 'for a black girl'?"

"I don't know," he said. He told himself, and me, that he just didn't know black girls, so he was color-blind. The same way I had done when I was actually color struck. It was good to go back to Pleasanton and see that I wasn't imagining what I felt as a kid. Once you're an adult, you can read the room in the context of the larger world. For some of these people, and definitely this guy, I was still the only black friend they had. That twenty years during which they could have found at least one replacement for me? Yeah, they never got to it. I looked around at the people gathered, standing around just like we did at the bonfires. How many black people had these people ever had in their homes? Did they work with any at all?

That's the thing, though. Having more black people around increases opportunities to learn and evolve, but that alone doesn't undo racist systems or thought processes. That is the real work we all have to do. I always want there to be a point to what I am saying, and I don't want to bring up the issue of colorism just to bring it up, or simply teach white readers about strife within the black community. At the very least, I of course want my friend to know she is not alone in her feelings about colorism. But I want to expect more than that. For years, we have advised women of color—light and dark—that the first step to healing is to acknowledge that colorism exists. Well, if we have hashtags about which teams people are on, black children staying out of the sun to avoid getting darker, and research studies that show the darker your skin, the greater your economic disadvantage, then we know colorism is a fact. We're ready for the next step, and we can't shrink from it just because it's hard and uncomfortable.

So let's aim higher than merely talking about it. Let's also expand that conversation beyond the black women who experience the damaging effects of colorism and stop telling them, "Love the skin you're in."

This cannot be a group hug of women validating women. Men must mentor girls as they grow into women, guiding them to find their own validation so they don't seek it elsewhere in negative ways. Tell your daughter or niece she is great and valued not in spite of who she is, but because she is exactly who she is. Because dark skin and Afrocentric features are not curses. We are beautiful. We are amazing and accomplished and smart.

Okay, smart is never a given with anyone, but we *are* here. And we don't need black ladies in airports and white guys in parking lots grading us on a curve, thank you very much.

nine

MISTLETOE GIRL #2 TELLS ALL

Ask any actor, and they will tell you the teacher who had the biggest influence on them as they crafted their technique. You'll hear names like Stanislavsky, Strasberg, Adler, Hagen, and, of course, my own teachers, Screech and Mr. Belding.

I made my screen debut with two lines as Mistletoe Girl #2 on *Saved by the Bell: The New Class*. And, yes, I was in awe of Dustin Diamond, aka Screech, and Dennis Haskins, aka Mr. Belding. All the other kids on set were as green as I was, but these two were veterans as the only holdovers from the original show. In this room, they were stars.

The show taped in front of a live studio audience, but during rehearsals the studio was empty. So any scene I wasn't in, which was the majority of them, I would go take a seat in the audience instead of going to my dressing room. I didn't just watch Dustin Diamond and Dennis Haskins act; I studied how they interacted with the director and how they treated the rest of the cast and the crew. Dustin had been doing comedy for years, so he had this slapstick ability that he would reserve and then tweak for scenes. I didn't realize that was a skill set you had to actually work at. Also, he was older than the teenagers on the show, and I knew I was going to be older than the people I was working with as long as I kept getting cast as a high schooler. Do you keep your distance as the adult? How much do you joke around? I literally just didn't know anything. And Dennis was all about dirty humor as soon as work was done, so I definitely learned that you could choose who you wanted to be on set.

I actually played two different black girls on the show, coming back later as Jennifer, a girl obsessed with collecting coins. She also inexplicably dressed like a 1950s housewife heading to a garden party, but then she went to the Sadie Hawkins dance in a hot red dress. I guess her closet had some serious range. I fortunately started my career off doing a lot of multicamera half-hour shows where I had the ability to sit in the audience and watch people work. One of my favorites to study was Sherman Hemsley on *Goode Behavior*, a house-arrest comedy. Yeah, a house-arrest sitcom. I tested to be a series regular as Sherman's granddaughter, but I didn't get the part. However, the producers brought me back to play her best friend. The whole time I was on set I was thinking, That's George Jefferson! I sat in the audience, listening to the notes he was given and watching how he tweaked his performance to suit them. It was a master class in comedic timing. Now, it wasn't my cup of tea, but he made it sound like it was. He had just the right rhythm to wait for the laugh and then zero in for the punch line.

My go-to acting technique was to smile a lot. The guy who

played Juan Epstein on *Welcome Back, Kotter,* Robert Hegyes, was one of the assistant directors. He saw me watching every scene and took a seat next to me out in the audience.

"I have two pieces of advice for you," he said.

I nodded and braced for the inevitable: "One, you're creepy. Two, stop staring at the talent."

"I can tell you're basically waiting for your line," he said. "It's 'Blah blah blah, now me.'"

He was right. Whenever I did a scene, I smiled a lot at the other actor to show I was listening, and almost nodded when it was about to be my turn, as if to say, "That's my cue."

"Always remember to listen to what the other actors are saying, and react. Just listen and react."

"Got it," I said. "Listen and react." I really did get it. One thing about me, I don't mind notes if they are helpful.

"The other thing to remember is this: you are always going to be able to find people who don't want to watch you fail."

He saw a young person who he knew was learning and took time to pull me aside and help me. Throughout my career, all kinds of people have been generous enough to help me and challenge me so they can see me be the best version of me. Hollywood is indeed dog-eat-dog, but there are groups of great people who are just nice. I held on to that, because this business also has a lot of rejection. When I first started auditioning for television shows, the main game was at Warner Bros., where everyone would hang out to audition for a shot on one of the million teen shows on the WB. I spent a lot of time doing guest spots on these series, playing high schoolers. In those rooms, there would be hundreds of other actors like me, dressed young even though we were all in our early to mid-twenties, but also honest-to-gosh kids. You could tell who they were because their mothers and fathers were grilling them on the material so hard that eventually the kid would have a crying meltdown. Mind you, this would be for a two-line gig on *Nick Freno: Licensed Teacher*.

As I got older and I spent more and more time on these sets, I realized these parents had given up everything else in their lives. So those two lines could decide whether or not they get to stay one more month at the Oakwood Apartments in Burbank, or had enough money to eat. A guy I met in those rooms, a successful actor now, told me what it was really like.

"Do you know me and my mom and my sisters were living out of my car during pilot season?" he asked me once. "We would get to the studio early and wash up in the bathroom there."

His mom had a trick when things got really bad. They would show up for the audition early and say that a younger sister had an accident. "Is there a trailer where we could wash her pants out?" she'd ask. Then they would go in the trailer and wash the family's clothes with hand soap.

"That's kind of ingenious," I said.

"It shows how badly they wanted it."

I was lucky in that I just wanted it for me. I became eligible to join the Screen Actors Guild (SAG) with an AT&T commercial directed by Forest Whitaker. I thought the ad was going to make me an ongoing AT&T spokesperson and thus rich, but the company scrapped it. But it was a union job, and if you are not union, that first job you book makes you union eligible. You cannot take a second union job without paying your dues. I was counting on paying my SAG dues with an ongoing gig on *Moesha*. I was supposed to play a head cheerleader, a nemesis to Brandy's Moesha. But they decided to not make the role recurring, and that was it. A job that was supposed to be a few episodes became just one: "Nah, we're good." I took that as being fired. How else was I supposed to take it? That always stayed with me. There's always someone bigger, badder, better. Don't save your best for when you think the material calls for it. Always bring your full potential to every take, and be on top of your job, or they will replace you.

PROBABLY 50 PERCENT OF THE FAN MAIL I'VE RECEIVED IN MY ENTIRE CAreer is because of one episode of *Star Trek: Deep Space Nine.* I played N'Garen in the "Sons and Daughters" episode, and Trekkies tell me that it was a pivotal one because it reintroduced Worf's son. My character had an interest in astrophysics, and as a rookie weapons officer for the Klingon Defense Force I took out a Jem'Hadar cruiser. Hadar's gonna hate.

The pivotal thing for me was that it was a job. I was twenty-four and I didn't want to play high schoolers forever. A Klingon, I thought, showed range.

We filmed at Stage 18 of Paramount's back lot, which was made to look like the IKS *Rotarran* hanging out on the Cardassian border. I see you, Trekkies. I'm not even going to make a Kardashian joke.

It took an obscene amount of time to turn me into a Klingon, and I would sit there for hours in the makeup chair, depleted of small talk because it took so long that there was simply nothing left to discuss. The hair and makeup room was huge, housing Ferengi ears and ridged Bajoran noses. My wig was standard Klingon, but fuller and somewhat braided, and for makeup I had just a hint of rose red on the lips. The look said warrior, but approachable. The irony of the situation was that the role was kind of high school: I was one of five new recruits, and Worf's son totally got bullied in the cafeteria. I was the mean girl of the squad.

The direction I kept getting was "Klingons don't smile." All day long I would get caught on camera with a grin. "Gabrielle, Klingons don't smile."

At lunchtime, I would stay in my makeup and a bunch of us Klingon recruits would go to Lucy's El Adobe Café on Melrose, across from Paramount Studios. The first time we went in, I expected *some* reaction.

"You must get a lot of Klingons, huh?" I asked.

"All kinds of people," said the waitress.

I ordered the ground beef tacos. As we Klingon day players sat there looking at the wall of autographed celebrity photos, I ate as much of the salsa as I could. To this day, I love their salsa.

On the last day, after working nineteen hours and escorting a convoy of Klingon cargo vessels to Donatu V, I was beat. They said I had to wait until the makeup department was ready so I could take my Klingon face off. I had an hour and a half to kill before they'd get to me. So I went back to Lucy's and sat alone in a booth with a book. Ricardo Montalbàn smiled down at me from an autographed picture. He was Khan on the original series and in *Star Trek II: The Wrath of Khan,* so it seemed like a sign. When the waiter came over, I ordered a margarita.

"Can I see some ID?"

He held my California license up to my Klingon face and squinted. "I don't know," he said. "You look different."

"It's me," I said.

"I know," he said. "I'm just kidding."

"Sorry," I said. "Klingons don't smile."

PRETTY SOON AFTER MY *DEEP SPACE NINE* GIG, I LANDED MY FIRST FILM: *10 Things I Hate About You.* Like a bunch of Klingon recruits, we all bonded that first night at the hotel in Tacoma, Washington. There wasn't a mean girl or boy among us, and we made a pact that this was going to be the best summer ever. There was Julia Stiles, wise beyond her New York years, and Joseph Gordon-Levitt, who was recognized everywhere he went as a star of NBC's *Third Rock from the Sun.* He and David Krumholtz—whom we affectionately called Krummy—bonded deep over their intellectual love of hip-hop. Larisa Oleynik was another child star, with her own show on Nickelodeon, and Andrew Keegan was the cast heart-throb. Susan May Pratt was a Michigan girl, and we clicked over our shared love of the Midwest and having a really, really good time. We were both the oldest. Playing a high schooler in your twenties isn't exactly mutton dressed as lamb, but it still makes you feel like people's big sister.

It was my first movie, this modern high school take on *Taming of the Shrew,* but we were all fish out of water. There was a "no favored nation" clause in all our contracts, which meant every cast member was treated equally. We all got the same type of hotel room, same rental car, and same type of trailer. That first week we had the run of Tacoma. It's a really beautiful port city, so we would go waterskiing and take camping trips. I made it my mission to make everyone laugh through a trip to Mount St. Helens. We were tight.

The new guy, someone named Heath Ledger from Australia, was set to show up a week into shooting. We were so afraid he was going to be a drag. Would he fit in? Would he be a jerk? Would he light up?

The first night after he arrived, he met us in the bar at the top of the hotel. Only Susan and I were over twenty-one, so the cast sent us up as ambassadors to check him out.

We found him, all of nineteen years old, drinking a scotch on the rocks and holding hands with his girlfriend, who appeared to be at least thirty-seven. He was stunning, with long dark hair falling in curls. Then he opened his mouth and he was James Bond.

"Hello, ladies," he said. He had this twinkle.

Susan and I looked at each other. Oh, this was going to work out just fine.

He talked about Shakespeare and art, all in an impossibly nondickhead way. He was two years out of Perth, which he described as "a wonderful place to grow up in as a kid, and a wonderful place to leave as a teenager." He was wise and sexy beyond his years.

We went downstairs to report our findings.

"What's he like?" everyone asked.

"He's a man," I said to the crew. "You're gonna love him."

And we did. Heath didn't have to try to ingratiate himself into our circle, which by then had turned our hotel into a sort of college dorm of smoking weed and big discussions about life. We were all within two floors of each other, and we would always end up in each other's rooms at the end of shooting, hanging out and listening to music. Heath would play the didgeridoo, a long cylindrical wind instrument he carried everywhere in a leather case. The sound is somewhere between a foghorn and an extended belch, but his passion for it was infectious. When hotel guests complained about the noise and the smell of weed, we acted very offended.

We also had a routine of eating together every night, and we'd often drive our little rental cars over to this joint that was like the local version of a Dave & Buster's for burgers and video games. The whole experience felt like the best summer camp.

When the cast moved up to Seattle, Julia's mom and Larisa's mom didn't want to stay, so they signed them over to me as the adult in charge. Bad move. (Sorry, moms!)

"First order of business," I told the girls, "is getting you fake IDs." Welcome to the Gabrielle Union Finishing School for Young Ladies.

We all went out as a pack in Seattle. Heath, ever the gentleman, held every door and our hands as we navigated the stairs of U-Dub college bars in our high heels. For me, it was fun to experience all of these adventures through their underage eyes. The rush of fake IDs! Beer! Throwing up! To add to the joy, there were lots of budding little romances among the cast, which were harmless and without drama.

When we wrapped, we knew for sure we would all see each other again, just like summer camp reunions. But that never happened. We were never all in the same place again. We all went right into new films except baby Larissa, who went straight off to college. I would see Julia on a plane, maybe Krummy. Andrew was such a club guy that I'd run into him here and there.

I don't want to overstate my own bond with Heath, because every single one of us shared it. Whenever I ran into him in L.A. after *10 Things,* it was like we had just wrapped yesterday. We would both reel off names of people from the movie that we had seen and share updates on their lives. There was never the weird Hollywood distance that creeps in. You usually get so close on a set and then it's out of sight, out of mind. You forget you were family for a while. Not this cast. Heath and I would hug and say, "Take care." His loss was a death in the family that all of us felt equally.

I'D PRETTY MUCH CORNERED THE MARKET ON OUTSPOKEN-BLACK-HIGH-schooler roles when I was invited to do a table read for a project called *Cheer Fever*. Honestly, the only reason I took the table read was that I had really wanted to get a role in *Sugar and Spice,* a bank-robbing-cheerleader film. I didn't get a spot in that one because, guess what, they didn't want to go black on any of the characters. And it bombed. It bombed so bad that I love telling people I didn't get the job, because it's like saying the Craigslist Killer never got back to you.

I was intrigued by the concept of *Cheer Fever,* which would of course become *Bring It On,* because it highlighted the rampant appropriation of black culture. Here, the idea was that a white high school squad, the San Diego Toros, get ahead by stealing cheer routines from a black team, the East Compton Clovers.

But when I got the script for the table read, my character, Isis, was a combination of Foxy Brown and eight other blaxploitation characters squeezed into a skintight cheerleader uniform. There were all these made-up slang words. Now, I am not the most Ebonically gifted person, but I recognize a made-up word when I see it.

The initial script had one word in particular, or, I should say, a collection of letters, that I just tripped over as I was reading it in my living room. I couldn't figure out what it said, so I showed it to my husband at the time. Chris peered at it like a word problem and then recoiled.

"Oh, God," he said.

"What?" I said. "What does it say?"

"I think they transcribed a *Martin* episode."

Martin Lawrence used to have these comic exclamations of disbelief as a realization dawned on him. It's an improv riff that he mastered, but they had tried to spell it out. The full line was

"Ossaywhattawhattawhat? Me-ow. *Me* gonna ow *you*. My nails are long, sharp, and ready to slash."

Clearly they were going for an Oscar. I love campy humor as much as the next person, but I didn't want to be picketed by the NAACP. The original script had Isis and Kirsten Dunst's character, Torrance, ending up cheering together at UC Berkeley. If you know what it takes to get into the UC system, you know Isis is not an ignorant fool. She's a leader, she's a great student, she's taking AP classes, and she's got high SAT scores. I wanted Isis to be presented as a tough leader who was not going to let these girls steal from her without some cheer justice for the act of cultural appropriation.

The director, Peyton Reed, was on board, and every morning we would meet in my trailer to rewrite dialogue to make it more believable. I could not, however, make my cheerleading skills seem at all believable. The actresses on the white squad, the Toros, had started filming earlier and had about three weeks of cheerleading camp to boot. Our squad, the Clovers, had nine days to learn the same number of routines. The Clovers consisted of three members of the girl group Blaque, several college cheerleaders, and me. Of course the pros and the girls from Blaque got it quickly, but me? I am not by any stretch a dancer, or someone who picks up eight counts quickly. So pretty much every day I would come into cheerleading camp smelling of Icy Hot, like somebody's old uncle.

Hi-Hat was our choreographer, and the poor thing knew I was hopeless. She just looked at me like, "Well, just do your best." I know she was thinking, This bitch is never gonna get it.

So they did a lot of close-ups of me during the routines. Wide shots were out because I don't match anybody.

One day I finally broke Hi-Hat. She threw up her hands.

"Do what you're gonna do," she said. "Just commit to it so it will look good."

Kirsten had a house with her mom out in La Jolla during that shoot, but the rest of the cast was staying in a San Diego hotel, going to all the bars and clubs around town. Everyone was horny, and there were a lot of marriages that didn't make it to the end of production. Normally I would be right in there for the fun, but I kind of felt like the cruise director. I was older and knew the area. There were a lot of people who weren't quite twenty-one yet and I couldn't get a million fake IDs. So the only place I could take them was Tijuana.

"How do you know TJ so well?" one cheerleader asked me, five tequilas in.

"I was on travel soccer in high school," I said. It's true. My soccer team was made up of the biggest female hellions in California. One time we walked across the border the night of an away game. We returned with one tattoo and six marines.

Kirsten was still in high school, and compared to me then she was *so* young. She was super nice and we would go out of our way to include her whenever we could. Her mom hosted barbecues, and we would all go because we wanted Kirsten to feel like part of the gang. You went, you ate, and you turned to the person next to you. "What bar are we going to?"

The movie came out and surprised everyone. We made ninety million dollars, and it's become a cult classic. Soccer dads will come up to me and start doing the cheers, the "Brrr, It's Cold in Here" routine, then ask me if they're doing it right. I have to answer, "Dude, I have no idea. Sorry."

I worked hard to make Isis a real character. It is interesting to me that when people reenact my scenes, they turn me back into that "Me-ow" caricature the director and I consciously took steps to avoid. They snap their fingers and say, "It's already been broughten."

That line is actually from a later spoof of teen movies, but perception is reality. Isis was an educated leader who refused to have her cheers stolen, but these people genuinely believe she was the villain.

A bunch of us did a cast reunion and photo shoot for a magazine a couple of years back. Kirsten was there and I mentioned how people say the "It's already been broughten" line at me even though it wasn't in the scene she and I played.

"It wasn't?" she said, laughing. "I thought it was."

Perception is reality.

SOMETIMES IT'S THE DIRECTOR'S PERCEPTION OF YOU THAT CAN RUIN A project. I get asked about *Friends* a lot because people know there were only two black people on the show who didn't play something like a waiter or Chandler's coworker. That leaves Aisha Tyler and me. For some reason, people get our plotlines confused. Aisha played the woman pursued by Joey and Ross. I played the woman pursued by Joey and Ross. Okay, I get it now.

When I was on, it was their seventh season, when *Friends* started to have more stunt guest stars. Susan Sarandon, Kristin Davis, Winona Ryder, Gary Oldman, and me.

I heard I got the gig on a Tuesday, the morning after my CBS hospital drama *City of Angels* was canceled. The best part of that show, by the way, was working with Blair Underwood—the sixth grader in me was dying. The worst part was having to yell "Pump in epinephrine!" and screwing it up each time. (*You* try it.) I had heard CBS gave great Christmas gifts, so my goal was to try to hang on until Christmas. We didn't make it.

When I drove onto the Warner Bros. lot I was not scheming to become best friends with the Friends. I was so okay with that. By then I had done 1,001 guest roles and I understood how these shows worked. If you're a regular, especially megastars grinding through your seventh season, you have so much on your plate that going out of your way to befriend your guest star is the last thing on the priority list.

But they were all really nice and totally professional. I thought, Okay, this could be cool. They had it down to a science and needed only three or four days to bang out an episode. My first scene was on the street outside Central Perk, with me unloading the back of a car, announcing that I am moving into the neighborhood. (Briefly, apparently.) The director was a regular, he did a lot of episodes. He went over the scene with David Schwimmer, Matt Perry, and the extras. Then he turned to me, and his tone completely changed.

"Do you know what a mark is?" he said in a singsong voice. "You stay on that so the camera can see you."

It was like he was talking to a toddler. He assumed on sight that I didn't know a single thing.

"Don't worry," I said. "I know."

Of course I knew what a mark was. Did he talk to other guest stars like this? The same thing happened in my next scene, this one with Matt LeBlanc.

"Okaaaay," the director continued in the singsong voice he reserved for me. He mimed how I should hold a lamp. "You could do thiiiiiis," he said. "Or thiiiiiiis."

His tone was so condescending, as if I had just wandered in off the street or won a contest for a *Friends* walk-on. It's funny, because I was standing there with Matt LeBlanc. I had four films under my belt that had either opened at number one at the box office or at number two behind blockbusters like the freaking *Matrix.* Matt, meanwhile, had made a movie with a monkey. Yet the director was talking to me, his guest star, as if I hadn't accomplished a single thing.

It's telling, I think, that my scenes were not in the usual *Friends* settings. First, I was outside Central Perk, a street set that fans know to be pretty rarely used on the show. Then Joey and Ross went inside Central Perk to discuss me, and then I showed up again with both of them at an obviously fake bar. My black face didn't darken the door of their favorite café, and certainly not the Friends' apartments. In their ninth year, Aisha Tyler had the weight of integrating the *Friends* set and storyline like some sort of Ruby Bridges of Must-See TV. They let her character, Charlie Wheeler, stay for nine episodes. In 2003, *Entertainment Weekly* suggested it was odd that the two black girls were given the exact same storyline. "The déjà vu wouldn't be that notable except that *Friends'* depiction of New York City is notoriously lily-white." Executive producer David Crane took umbrage. "The other story line [with Union] was quick and funny, where the two guys didn't realize they were dating the same girl," he told the magazine. "Charlie Wheeler [Tyler] is a brilliant paleontologist who should be dating someone like Ross, but hooks up with Joey first." Got it.

By 2016, the whitewashing of the Friends' world was so apparent in reruns and streaming that series cocreator Marta Kauffman had to acknowledge the situation to the *Washington Post.* "That is a criticism we have heard quite a bit," Kauffman said. "When we cast the show, we didn't say to ourselves, 'This is going to be an all-white cast.'"

But it was. I didn't call the director on the way he treated me, which I regret. I thought, *No wonder you don't have black talent on this show.* He assumed I didn't know anything and he felt comfortable dismissing me with condescending directives. It's actually not enough to just point out that there were so few black actors on the show. We need to look at why, *and* why it was assumed that I knew nothing. Bias, whether implicit or explicit, hits every industry. To be a black person is to understand what it is to be automatically infantilized and have it be assumed that you don't have the talent or the skill set required to do your job. It's the reason Dr. Tamika Cross, a chief resident and OB/GYN, was stopped from helping a man who fell unconscious on her flight. When they asked if there was a doctor who could help, Tamika went into action. And was denied.

"Oh, no, sweetie," Dr. Cross recalled the flight attendant saying. "Put your hand down, we are looking for actual physicians or nurses or some kind of medical personnel; we don't have time to talk to you."

To compare myself to a doctor is a leap, I know, but it's just how people talk to us. So no, I couldn't possibly know where my mark was.

My short time on the *Friends* set was a lesson, though. I had grown as an actress, raised my salary quote, and proved I could open films. But it wasn't enough. I thought about that speech Dad gave me before I started elementary school: "You're gonna have to be bigger, badder, better, just to be considered equal. You're gonna have to do twice as much work and you're not going to get any credit."

It was still true, even in the land of make-believe.

ten

CRASH-AND-BURN MARRIAGE

Have you ever had a dream where you're in a car and you're heading right for a wall? You're trying to hit the brakes, but you just speed closer and closer to your doom? Well, you are cordially invited to my first wedding.

May 5, 2001, was a hot day, even for New Orleans. My bridesmaids were all hungover, their faces puffy and shiny from frozen daiquiris and hurricanes, a peril of having your wedding during Jazz Fest. Just before the ceremony, they were rock-paper-scissoring to see who got to go down the aisle with the Heisman winners. The loser had to walk with the groom's friend who was just sprung from jail. He'd made bail in a murder case and was still wearing prison braids, as fuzzy as his alibi.

Their game of rock-paper-scissors was a convenient distraction from what I was pretty sure could be a heart attack. But once they all walked, it was just me, myself, and my anxiety, standing at the beginning of an aisle that now seemed a country mile long. At the end was Chris, someone I had no business marrying.

I took a step, and my shaking started with the first chords of "Endless Love." I was on the edge of sobs, but not the usual wedding tears of a bride overcome by emotion. Everyone could tell, especially my father. He looped his arm through mine to escort me, which is to say drag me, down the aisle.

"Stop it," he hissed in my ear. "Stop this right now. You're back at Foothill High School. You're the point guard; you're leading your team. Stop this foolishness."

I nodded, trying to turn my ugly-cry into a game face. Two guests I didn't recognize jumped in front of the videographer to take photos. They paused a beat, each lowering their disposable cameras and smiling as if giving direction. Like maybe I'd get the idea and be happy. Chris and I hadn't thought to write the number of guests allowed on the response card, so our wedding planner had simply seated, say, fifteen people on a card that went to one cousin. "The girl from *Bring It On* is marrying that football player, so invite the whole block," I imagine them saying. "Well, yeah, he got cut from the Jacksonville Jaguars, but he's hoping to be a Raider."

As Dad held me up down the aisle, I saw that the pastor that Chris's mother had insisted we use was not there. My family is Catholic, but Chris wouldn't commit to doing the Pre-Cana classes you have to take in order to get married by a priest. His mother's suddenly precious pastor had skipped the rehearsal. I thought if he was a no-show, that would be my out. Then I saw him, blending in and chatting with the groomsmen. Mingling at my wedding ceremony.

I had asked one of my closest guy friends, Dulé Hill, to do

a reading. He was playing Charlie on *The West Wing* at the time, and I had been his girlfriend on the show. Dulé thought this marriage was a terrible mistake, so as he read from Corinthians, he kept sighing dramatically, pausing to look at me like, "Are you getting this?"

"Love is patient," he said, "*love* is kind."

After an eye roll, he continued, ticking off all the boxes on what was wrong with my relationship.

"It does not envy, it does not boast, it is not proud. It does not dishonor others."

Long pause. Tick. Tick. Tick.

I heard a plane in the distance.

"It is not self-seeking, it is not easily angered, it keeps no record of wrongs."

If Chris and I had kept no record of wrongs, we would have had nothing to talk about. His endless cheating had given me permission to cheat, too. I was just less sloppy about it, so he wasn't aware. While he dealt in volume, I dealt in quality. A note for the novice cheater: never, ever cheat with someone who has less to lose than you. You want someone who will be more inclined to keep his or her mouth shut.

"Who gives this woman to be married to this man?" the pastor asked, his voice thick with Louisiana country. Chris suddenly turned his back on me. I remember it in slow motion, him stepping down from the altar and moving toward his groomsmen.

I was being left at the altar, I thought. This was really happening. I had missed my chance to run, and now *he* was Julia freaking Roberts, the Runaway Groom riding off on a horse. He knows, I thought. He knows I cheated on him and he won't marry trash.

Chris leaned in with his groomsmen, taking a huddle. They stamped their feet in unison, all turning back to me with a football chant of "We do!"

It was a joke. Chris had planned this. He wasn't leaving me. He didn't know I was trash. I was saved from shame and washed with relief. I could endure a toxic marriage, but the humiliation of being left, of being publicly rejected—that would have been too much.

The pastor began the vows. "Do you, Gabriel, take Christopher to be your lawfully wedded husband?"

Wait, I thought. "Gabriel"? This guy just mispronounced my name at my own wedding? But I was raised to never correct people. Certainly not a pastor. All I needed to do was say my name the right way when I repeated the vows. But because I was a good Catholic girl, I said it wrong.

"I, Gabriel, take . . ."

A groan went up from the bridesmaids. I glanced back at their disbelieving faces, then over at Dulé, ready with the faintest shake of his head. I smiled at Chris, which is something I always do to another actor when I am nervous in a scene and just want to get through it. I had a hard time looking at him, so my eyes settled on his forehead.

The pastor pronounced us man and wife, and our exit song down the aisle was Natalie Cole's "This Will Be." It's a cockeyed ode to bliss that now seems a little too on the nose irony-wise. Our videographer walked backward in front of us, capturing the exact moment one of our groomsmen, a huge guy named Zeus, clapped us on the back.

"Y'alls is married now," he said, riffing on a *Color Purple* line with a voice full of forced wonder and excitement.

On the video, which I have watched only once, you see my face fall. It was the beginning of the end.

SO WHAT GOT ME THERE? WELL, MY ROOMMATE IN 1999 HAD A THING FOR linebackers in the AFC Central Division. Her taste was very specific, and I can't fault her for it because they were actually all great guys. One in particular hosted a three-day party in Jacksonville, Florida, every April. My roommate and I went one year with some friends, and on the first night there was a bowling party. I immediately clocked this guy in the next lane, definitely not my type. He was a running back, short and built, and a Jacksonville Jaguars teammate had given him the nickname "Little Thicky." That was an accurate description. He had on these baggy jeans, and he'd cut off the hems to shorten them. Later, when I was shopping for him, I learned that 38-28 is in fact a mean size to find.

"What are you, Huck Finn?" I asked, looking down at his frayed cuffs.

"My name's Chris."

"Where's Jim? He out watching the raft?"

He gave it right back, trash-talking my game. He was legit funny, a country boy from Kenner, Louisiana, where they take turtles out of the swamp to cook them. He liked drinking dark liquor and playing cards, and he reminded me of the kind of men who married into my family. The contrast was that he also had tattoos all over his arms, two earrings, and an easy cartoon cat smile. When we were all leaving, he got on a Ducati, and that sealed it. As a child of *Grease 2,* I was always on the lookout for a Cool Rider.

I found myself thinking about him, and the next night he showed up at the house where most of us were staying. One of my girlfriends was like, "He's *downstairs*!" He had come back, so that meant he was interested, too. It's funny, in retrospect, how excited I was.

We spent the rest of the party weekend joined at the hip, hanging out and trading potshots. A big part of our courtship was ragging on each other. Sure, later we would use it as a weapon, having learned what to say to wound and what would be the kill shot. But in the beginning, it was good fun. It felt like a mutual chase.

We would visit each other in Jacksonville and L.A. for weekends. My career was starting to rise, so the arrangement was good. I could focus on work and auditions while he did his training. We had dreams. "After football, I'm one class away from my kinesiology degree from Michigan," he told me. "I want to go into sports medicine."

In July, after three months of dating, Chris bought an engagement ring, but he held on to it until my birthday, at the end of October. I flew to Jacksonville to celebrate. I spent the whole day at the spa, and when I got back to his house, there was a rose petal path from the front door to the bedroom. At the end was Chris, down on one knee. He had a bucket of KFC on the floor, and he was eating KFC potato wedges with one hand while holding a ring in the other. When I tell this story to new girlfriends, they always ask, tentatively, if there was some sentimental thing about KFC. No, I have to tell them; in the first of a list of many ignored red flags, I guess he was eating and I had surprised him.

The ring felt big and special, and so many of my friends were already married. I'd won something under the wire, I thought. I was the girl who called everyone to share my news, but I remember feeling more and more apprehensive with each call. I'm the opposite of impetuous. I am a "measure sixteen times, then cut once" person. And then torture myself in the middle of the night about how I kind of did a half-assed job on that sixteenth measurement. So I got defensive when the general response was "Are you sure?" and "As long as you're happy . . ." People thought it was a terrible idea, given that I'd only known him a few months and had only seen him on random weekends. People on the other side of marriage know what happens when you've never spent any real time together. I had no idea what that reality actually looked like, but I told myself I was just efficient.

The next day I had to fly up to Wilmington to audition for *Dawson's Creek*. It was a quick trip, there and back in one day. Back in Jacksonville, I let myself into Chris's place while he was still at practice and got on his computer to check my e-mail.

Kids, this was medieval times, when olde-timey laptops used to have messages pop up on the screen like they were breaking in with a special report. And there it was:

"Yo, you still got that girl coming in next weekend? Nigga, she's Greek. Nigga, she's Greek."

This was from his best friend. Now, I am not Greek. Nor do I know why his friend was so insistent about this woman's Greek identity. All I knew was that I was going to be back in L.A. the weekend of Greekfest. And this was literally not even twenty-four hours after he had proposed to me.

I packed my bag and kept my ring on just so he could see me take it off when I threw it at him. When he walked in the door, I nailed it, throwing the diamond right at him. Chris entered the scene in full apology mode, as his boy had tipped him off. I guess my reply—something like "Yes, what was her name again?"—gave away that the person typing wasn't Chris. He bent to pick up the ring and was crawling on the ground, begging.

"You *just* proposed," I yelled.

"I didn't know if you were going to say yes," he said.

"So you lined up a backup?" I yelled. "Who do you think you're kidding?"

But for someone with an intense fear of public humiliation, who, just hours ago, felt lucky to have been chosen, I had no choice but to stay. I didn't have it in me to call all those people twenty-four hours later to say, "You were right." Because then everyone would know just how naïve and foolish I really was.

The judgment, I imagined, would be on a grand scale. My publicist had also announced our engagement to the press, and I felt like there was no turning back. People had taken time to ask my publicist for details on how we met and I had already crafted a quote about our happiness. "Yeah, about what I said," I dreaded saying. "Uh, please respect our privacy during this difficult time?" Now I know the headline would have been "Eighth Lead of *She's All That* Calls Off Engagement," but in my mind, the story was far bigger.

I stalled, putting off sending out the Save the Dates and stretching the engagement from 1999 all the way to 2001. When the Jaguars cut him in 2000, my girlfriends told me that I should, too. But I couldn't kick him while he was down. I also believed he had a real skill set that would be attractive to another team. The Raiders were interested, and by the time we finally got married, he was doing off-season training with them. He was technically on the team and got a small stipend for working out, but he didn't have a contract. We married in May, and at the end of August he got cut from the Raiders and never played football again. And for the rest of our marriage, never had another check. From a job. Ever again.

What about that kinesiology degree he was so close to getting? Funny, I asked the same question.

"Yeah, about that," he said. "I'm actually a year and a half away. And if you're an ex-athlete on scholarship and don't tell the university that you want to come back in a certain amount of time, they don't budget for you. I'd be paying for it. Since I don't live in Michigan, I'd be paying out-of-state tuition."

So the Bank of Gabrielle Union was officially open. And doing a brisk business.

I TRIED. NOT MUCH, MIND YOU. BUT I DID TRY. WE WERE LIVING IN A cookie-cutter split-level town house in the Tarzana neighborhood of L.A., and he decided he needed office space for a company that (as far as I could tell) existed mainly in his mind. He'd convinced a few people to hire him as a marketing-type consulting person of some sort and he was adamant he needed a plush office to be taken seriously. So I got him one by the Fox lot in Century City. He needed to have that office feng-shuied, by the way. Never been to Asia, but he needed it to be feng-shuied to be on trend. I thought, If this is what will make you happy and productive, you do you. Neither happened.

I started handing him ways to make me happy, gradually making them simpler and simpler. "What was the name of that soul food place we saw on Sepulveda?" I'd ask. "Maybe we should go there some night."

He upped his game, however, as a prolific cheater. I was resigned to it, more annoyed by his moping around than his cheating. I'd hear the garage door and tense up, not sure what mood he'd be in. I distinctly remember yelling, "I don't care who sucks your dick, just come home and be nice to me."

Yet I would suddenly decide to get randomly, epically jealous. I was doing laundry one day and going through his pockets. Since it wasn't his money he was running around with, he could always be counted upon to put cash or credit cards through the wash. Sitting cross-legged on our bedroom floor, I found a piece of paper reading ANGELINA, 818-whatever-whatever.

The ragey-rage set in. I knew he was fucking other people, but finding that number set me off. I decided to stash the number on top of the armoire in our bedroom, where it sat, waiting for the perfect moment for me to go ballistic when he accused me of something. Exhibit A: You're a dick. Prosecution rests. Case closed.

It took a couple of weeks, but sure enough, he handed me just the right opportunity to go for it. I pulled down the number.

"Is this the bitch?" I screamed, sounding like Rowdy Roddy Piper from the WWF. "Angelina? Is this the bitch you're fucking?"

He laughed. Right in my face. I became unhinged, fueled by embarrassment and anger.

"You think you're gonna call this bitch?" I screamed. "YOU THINK YOU'RE GONNA CALL THIS BITCH?"

Reader, I put the paper in my mouth. I chomped and chewed until I could swallow.

"You're not calling this bitch," I said, coughing a little.

Chris paused. "Angelina is the name of the soul food restaurant you asked me to find."

I blinked. "Well," I said.

"How does that taste?"

Another time we went nine days straight without speaking. Ghosts in a split-level house, finding reasons not to be in the same room. In the midst of this, I had a red-carpet premiere that involved some sort of love theme, so I needed a date. Reporters had been picking up a "trouble in paradise" vibe with us, and I thought I had to keep up appearances.

Hours before the event, he was downstairs watching TV and I was upstairs thinking, How do I even get him to talk to me? And I hatched a plan I am not proud of. "I bet if I was injured he would have to talk to me."

I went to the middle landing and then down a couple steps. By that time, I had done a couple of action movies, so I knew how to fake a fall without being injured. I tucked and rolled, slamming the wall where I knew he was sitting on the other side.

"Baby!" he said, running to me.

"Don't you baby me," I said, screaming and pretending to fight back tears. I pulled out the performance of my life. "You don't even want to talk to me and now I've got to go to this premiere all alone and I'm *injured*."

He went to the premiere. We smiled for the cameras. We played our roles.

My drama moves weren't always successes. Like the night I ran away from home. Yes, my adult home. You know the moment in the movies where the girl runs off and the guy runs after her? Well, I tried my hand at that. Midfight, I literally ran out of my own house in shorts and a T-shirt. No wallet, no phone. I just started running, assuming Chris was going to run after me. But I forgot that I was in decent shape, so I just kept going.

I ended up on the backside of a park, one where he played basketball. He'll come find me here, I thought. I propped myself against a tree and waited. Just so we could have this scene of "Thank you for finding me . . ."

He never came. Instead, I fell asleep, sitting against a tree.

I woke up to the tingling feeling of a trail of ants climbing up my arm.

Hello, rock bottom, I thought.

It was after 4 A.M. and the sun was just starting to creep up. I had run so far from home that now I had to walk back. Step after step of utter Charlie Brown defeat. I held on to the glimmer of hope that Chris would be waiting at the door, frantic. I planned out my apology to the police, who I was certain would be swarming my house after Chris's call about a missing person. "I just needed some air."

When I got home Chris was fast asleep up in our room, snoring to the heavens. He could not be bothered.

You are right to wonder if we sought professional help. There were indeed forays into couples therapy. The first one, we had the luxury of choice. We were on the *Titanic,* asking to see the bar menu. We decided we wanted a black woman, and a Christian woman at that. We thought she would shame us into being together. Fifteen minutes into our first session, before we even got to any of the tough stuff, she stopped us.

"This isn't gonna work," she said. "You guys don't belong together."

We'd been dumped.

"How dare she?" I scoffed before we even got in the car.

"Who does she think she is?" snapped Chris.

Oh, we were going to show that woman. Things got better for a bit, in that every once in a while we would have a great night where we laughed. Maybe this is enough, I thought.

Our friends didn't think so. One sent us to another therapist named Sally, whom our friend credited with saving her marriage. Like the good Christian sister therapist before her, Sally also marveled how we ever got past the dating stage, but she was committed.

We lied to Sally constantly. Chris and I were both terrified of being judged. When one of us would go out on a limb and share some uncomfortable truth, the other person would act blindsided. My eyes would widen like I couldn't begin to comprehend where any of this was coming from. I wanted Sally to like me, so I couldn't tell her the truth. I wanted to win.

Sally called me on my competitiveness pretty early in our sessions. "You think in terms of winning and losing," she said. "But if you're winning, who's losing?"

"Him!"

"That's your husband," she said slowly, like this might be news to me. "You're not supposed to want him to lose."

"Wow," I said. "You don't know me, huh?"

Chris decided to stop coming to the appointments. I kept right on like the good student I was, needing that A.

"Now that we're here alone, you need an exit strategy," she said, leaning in. "Why don't you give yourself six months to mentally, physically, financially, prepare to leave."

Sally was talking truth now. I kept going alone, and I started to get a plan together. There was an actual date in my calendar, and the date came and went. I knew the milk was not just spilled all over the floor, it had been left out to curdle. And I was spooning it up, saying, "I can still eat cereal with this."

THEN CAMERON CAMERA ENTERED MY LIFE. THAT'S NOT HER REAL NAME— her working name was even dopier—and I resent protecting the identity of a woman who tried to extort me after sleeping with my husband, but I am not sure of the etiquette.

Chris and I went to a summer potluck with a bunch of couples. There was this woman there, serving up Sexy Librarian and being very flirty with all the husbands. At one point, a bunch of guys were missing, and I found her showing them all her Web site, Cameron Camera, where people paid to watch her in various stages of undress. Great potluck, everyone! Gentlemen, hide your hard-ons!

A lot of people wanted to go out after the potluck night, including Chris, but I had a girlfriend drive me home. He ended up hooking up with Cameron Camera in our SUV. And of course she left an earring, probably one she got ten-for-a-dollar at a pharmacy for just such occasions. That gave her the excuse to call him at his office—the one I got feng-shuied—which gave him the excuse to have sex with her again. "Since you came all the way out to Century City, the least I can do is fuck you."

Cameron Camera laid low for quite some time, surfacing when she heard I had the *Honeymooners* movie coming out. She contacted a bunch of tabloids and entertainment news shows, saying she was ready to sell proof that Gabrielle Union's husband was cheating.

A friend at one of the shows gave my team a heads-up. Before telling me about the woman, they hired Marty Singer, legal guard dog and bad cop to the stars. I was downstairs in my dining room when my cell phone rang. At the other end were my agent, my manager, my publicist, and special guest star Marty.

"Listen," my manager said, "this is a really hard conversation to have . . ."

Oh God, I thought, they're dropping me.

"I'll just say it," he said. "Someone is shopping around a story that Chris is cheating on you. She has photos."

"Oh," I said quietly, then louder. "Oh." And I laughed. I howled.

"Gabrielle . . ." said my publicist.

"Which woman?" I asked. Chris was upstairs, and I spoke to the ceiling. "Trust me, this isn't a problem."

"Her name is Cameron," said my publicist.

"Oh, Cameron Camera with the nudie site," I said, blurting it out like a charades answer to show how cool I was with this. "She's not even cute. I'm so sorry she bothered you. Please don't worry."

"It might not be so easy," my agent said. "You have a movie coming out. We need to know what the pictures are so we can warn the studio."

"Like if it's kissing, whatever," said my manager. "If it's her hand up his ass . . ."

"Got it," I said. "Hand up the ass is a problem."

"So we need to see what she has," said Marty. "Set up a sting and put a price on those photos. In the meantime, talk to Chris and see what she has on him."

Like he was waiting for his cue, Chris came down the stairs. The same ones I'd "fallen down" a few months before.

"You didn't notice the flashbulbs?" I asked.

"What?"

"When she was taking pictures of you guys fucking, you didn't notice the flash going off?"

"What?" Maybe he was in straight denial or, like me, was trying to figure out which woman it could have been.

"Cameron Camera, remember her?" I said, casually, like I was jogging his memory. "You fucked her last summer? Well, she waited for just the right moment. Now she's gone to all these people saying she has proof that you cheated. Anything you want to say?"

Just like how we began, when he got caught with the Greek, he went right into groveling.

"Get out!" I screamed. "I'm about to have to pay a bitch for fucking my husband. *And* I have to pay Marty Singer to help me pay her! Your dick keeps costing me money!"

He was panicked, but not about losing a wife. If I left, the cash flow would go with me, and with it the illusion of his success.

I became fixated on the word "sting," which they set up that week for 7 A.M. in a coffee shop. All the intrigue made the situation sound at least slightly more exciting than just asking, pretty please, to see exactly what position the woman was in with my husband. I kept my phone in my hand all morning, but Cameron Camera never showed. Either she didn't really have proof and didn't think we'd ask to see it in exchange for the money, or she just wanted to feel relevant.

My marriage was obviously over, but I was still desperately afraid of people labeling me a failure, so I didn't want to jump right into the divorce, either. Carrie Fisher had a line I love about why she and Paul Simon ended their marriage: "Things were getting worse faster than we could lower our standards." I realized that I needed to really take stock of the situation between Chris and me, and make a decision based not in anger but in what I really wanted and how I really felt.

So one night, I was sitting up in our bed when he came in the room.

"Let's talk," I said.

"Yeah," he said.

"Listen," I said, "if we're gonna have this conversation, let's be brutally honest."

"Okay," he said, sitting down next to me. "The truth."

We went through it, question by question, bringing up even the most obscure things from years prior. “When you said you got into a fight at Mel’s Diner in Hollywood,” I asked, “was that true?”

“No,” he said. “I was with somebody.”

“You went through the motions of tearing your shirt?”

“Yeah.”

“I knew it,” I said, laughing. “The way it was torn, I knew it.”

He brought up an actor I had done a film with.

“Did you sleep with him?” he asked.

“No,” I said.

“Were you in love with him?”

“Yes,” I said. “Yes, I was. But you would have been in love with him, too.”

There was something about the permission to be honest that allowed us to reestablish the friendship we had in the beginning. That night we decided to split up, and yet in the months after, we became sort of best friends again. We hung out more in those months than when we were married. Before, we had been that downer couple that ruined the party when we showed up. It was that uncomfortable to be in our presence. But as separated people, our friends were like, “Hey, we can hang!”

When we announced the separation, my team gave a statement to the AP at 9 A.M. West Coast time. By 9:15, my publicist and manager started what they called “The Divorce List.” Reps for athletes and celebrities were calling to see if they could set up a date. Some were reaching out directly.

My manager called to tell me I was popular.

“Who?” I said, pretending to be disgusted but feeling flattered. “Who wouldn’t give me a *day*?”

He reeled off the first two, naming an aging sportscaster and then maybe a fading music producer who held on to his Jheri curl two decades too long.

"Okay," I said. "I'm good. Please stop."

The honeymoon period of my divorce from Chris was short-lived, and I did the laundry list of dumb things you do when you want your ex to like you. I invested in a company he started with one of my friends. I paid rent for six months on a new home for him and cosigned for a Porsche. Then he abandoned the Porsche at the Burbank airport and I inherited a bunch of bills and parking tickets. The business failed, so there went that money, too. And like my money, I have never seen him again.

Chris moved to Atlanta, where I shoot *Being Mary Jane*. I reached out to him once and said, "Let's get together." I meant it, but he owes me so much money, I'm afraid he thought it was a trap. He never showed.

He needn't worry. My sting days are behind me.

eleven

PRESCRIPTION FOR A BREAKUP

Are you experiencing heartbreak accompanied by nutty behavior?

Symptoms include, but are not limited to, obsessively clocking your ex's social media and light stalking of the new girl's Instagram. You may also be having moderate to severe instances of driving past their house and hiding in their bushes. You have been given a diagnosis of generally crazy, unproductive behavior.

I am here to help. What I can prescribe is not medication, but an easy-to-follow syllabus and wine list. This is a list of pro tips best used NOW.

PRO TIP: WATCH *SPLENDOR IN THE GRASS*

Shot in luscious Technicolor, *Splendor in the Grass* is Warren Beatty's first film and one of Natalie Wood's best. She plays Deanie, a pre-Depression Kansas girl who understandably falls in lust and love with Warren's Bud. He loves her, too, but has sex with been-there-done-that Juanita instead. Deanie wants to have sex with Bud so badly that repressing the desire drives her insane. Everyone who I make watch this film remembers this one doozy Deanie tosses out during her mad scene in the bathtub: "Did he spoil me? No. No, Mom! I'm not spoiled! I'm not spoiled, Mom! I'm just as fresh and I'm virginal like the day I was born, Mom!"

My mom loved Natalie Wood, so I grew up watching this film and her others, like *West Side Story* and *Rebel Without a Cause.* Junior year of high school, I needed *Splendor in the Grass* to help get me through my first, and perhaps worst, breakup. Only then was I able to fully understand Deanie and feel understood myself. She and I knew the truth: heartbreak feels like a death sentence.

I thought Jason Kidd and I were a power couple. He was a sophomore at a nearby Catholic high school, quickly becoming a national phenom. But part of the allure for me was that he seemed like such a good guy. He came from a two-parent household and he was Catholic like me. We had this very eighth-grade relationship, despite being in high school. We didn't have sex. I had already lost my virginity, so I was down for it, but it didn't seem like something he had to have in order to be with me.

Two weeks before my junior prom, I went to one of his games. My friends couldn't go and I didn't want to do the thirty-minute drive from Pleasanton by myself, so I asked my dad if he would come along. He loved that I was dating Jason, so that was a no-brainer for him. We sat in the stands, and I saw his parents were in the bleachers across the gym. Next to them was a tall girl with an asymmetrical haircut like Salt's from Salt-N-Pepa, only even shorter on one side and longer on the other. I took her to be a cousin or family friend. She was wearing Jason's #32 wristband, and I thought, *How sweet. He gave his cousin his wristband.*

Then I noticed that he was wearing a #22 wristband. When you as a player wear someone else's jersey number it means one of two things: You are paying tribute to a significant other who plays, or you are honoring a player who died. Now, my number was 21, so I made up this scenario in my head about who #22 could be. My teenage levels of narcissism and drama wrapped in a crazy double helix of denial. I decided Jason had a friend who died. Jason was so sensitive, paying homage to this person via a sweatband. RIP #22, I hardly knew you.

During the game, a few of his friends came over to me, led by a female friend of his with a severe case of a Valley Girl accent. "Soooo, are you and Jason going to prom?" she asked.

"Yeah," I answered, innocently.

"Uhhhhmmmmm, I might, like, hold off on those plans."

I flew right past the obvious dig. Why would Jason be busy? We had talked about prom. He's didn't have a game. Clueless Valley Girl.

Then, a guy friend of his came up to me.

"Hey, you know, whatever happens with you and Jason," he said, pausing for a second, "you know, we're always gonna be friends. *I* think you're really cool."

"Oh," I said. "Okay."

See this is what grown-up love was about. You created connections with his friends. And even though you know you will never, ever break up—because that would be preposterous, right?—you keep those friendships you made. I filed that knowledge away for a time I would never, ever need it.

Jason's team won, and right after the game ended the high school gymnasium ritual of pushing in all the bleachers began. Jason was already doing postgame interviews in high school, so they had left one of the bleachers open for the entire team to sit and wait for him. He was literally surrounded by a ring of reporters. And at six foot four as a sophomore in high school, he was head and shoulders above the crop of people jotting down what he said. I could clearly see his face as I stood standing off to the side with my dad. Across from us, pointedly not saying hello, were Jason's parents and this girl "cousin."

Then his teammates started a chant:

"Just do it, you pussy. Just do it." Over and over, and Jason kept looking at me and then back at the team and then back at me.

My dad smelled what was coming. "We should go, Nickie," he said, as if the idea had just occurred to him. "We should just get out of here."

"Just do it, you pussy," the chant continued. "Just do it."

"We need to talk," Jason yelled to me over the reporters. They all turned to look at me.

The chant stopped, and the gym was silent except for the squeaks of sneakers as his teammates leaned forward in anticipation.

"Let's go, Nickie," Dad said.

"No, Dad," I said, in my most dramatic voice. "I want to know the truth."

But I couldn't let go of hope.

"Um, is it positive?" I said, giving the thumbs-up sign. "Or is it negative?"

Jason gave a thumbs-down sign. The team went "OHHHHHHH!" in unison.

Condemned to death by heartbreak, I ran from the arena.

He called me that night to officially break up with me, which is exactly what he had done to the girl he dated before me. Karma is a bitch that surfaces quickly. I went into this very quick whirlpool of a downward spiral. I began writing a lot of sad, terrible poetry. I even incorporated my vocabulary words into the verse with lines like "You are the crystal sextant leading me to my fate." Then there was a poem I called "Little Boys."

Little boys like to play
Childish games from night to day.
They think they're grown, but to their dismay
They're years from where manhood and maturity lay.

The fact that I remember this, thirty years later, speaks volumes about where I was at that time. It's just one from a full three-ring binder of musings on my despair. I asked myself if #22 gave Jason more than I did as #21? Just as Deanie tortured herself over Juanita, I wonder if I had been naïve to think he didn't want sex. Was that the deal breaker? 'Cause, jeez, tell a girl.

I also had the terrible realization that I now had two weeks to find a date for fucking prom. I'd just been dumped by Jason Kidd, so it had to be a *good* date.

There was another black kid that had moved to Pleasanton, a guy named Walter. He was a senior when I was a junior, and he was the running back on the football team. He was really cute, and I decided his looks alone made him my best candidate. Even though my heart was still broken, the pictures would tell a different story. As one of my girlfriends said, "The pictures are going to last a lot longer than your memory."

My vanity about the optics was so consuming, I even convinced myself I had a crush on him. It was him all along. To hell with Jason. I just had to actually talk to Walter first. I decided that the best way to not take another hit to my dignity was to ask him in the most casual, devil-may-care way. If I just ran into him and tossed it off . . .

Walter lived in the Val Vista development, right at the entrance to a cul-de-sac. Saturday afternoon I decided to do a drive-by in my mom's Cutlass Ciera. I went by the house and didn't see anybody around. I was relieved and realized that this was a fool's mission. Worse, I realized that the problem with doing a drive-by in a cul-de-sac is that it's actually two drive-bys. I went around the circle, and as I was a few houses down from passing again, his garage door started to open. Shit.

I gunned the engine and saw his dog flying down the driveway. This crazy dog ran right in front of my car! And I panicked: the teen driver in her mom's Cutlass hit the gas instead of the brake. The last thing I saw was his dog jumping for my mom's hood ornament.

I braked again and looked behind me. The dog was running in circles, fine. He had crouched under my car as I ran over him. Stunt dog. I pulled over and had the shakes. I just did a drive-by of my faux crush's house and almost crushed his dog.

Lesson learned, I just called him. I didn't tell him I was only choosing him for the optics. And karma got me. A week before prom, Walter got the goddamned chicken pox. He was no longer contagious on the big night, but he was covered head to toe in chicken pox scabs.

Through *Splendor in the Grass,* I also saw the way out. In the film—spoiler alert!—Deanie tries to kill herself and her parents have her institutionalized. This is the part you need to see, my brokenhearted one: While she's locked up, Bud goes to Yale and completely blows it. His family loses everything when the stock market crashes and he has to come home and work the ranch. Deanie, sprung from the nuthouse, gets a new dude and goes to see Bud. She's got her rich girl gloves on and she's at their filthy farm with chickens everywhere. There's Bud, working with his dirty hands and hanging out with his new girl, who looks like a mess. You see it in Deanie's face: Whew, I dodged a bullet.

So I say to my patients, the friends going through a bad split, "You are Deanie." We waste our nutty on people who don't deserve it. Wait it out. He's gonna end up dirty with chickens and #22, and you're going to come out on top. Trust me on this one.

PRO TIP: WATCH *WAITING TO EXHALE* AND LIVE IN THE SOUNDTRACK

This is for when things get really messy, as they did for me in my early twenties when I couldn't wait for my Greek-Mexican beauty school dropout to break up with me, and then would do anything to get him back.

Alex and I had moved to L.A. together, against the wishes of his parents, who called him a nigger lover. So there was that little hurdle. I was still at UCLA, and I used my own student loan and my Payless settlement money to finance his beauty school tuition. I hated the Payless money and saw it as blood money, payment for being put in an unsafe situation that allowed me to be raped. Alex had no problem with taking that money, and in many ways saw it as something he had a right to because of what, he said, *we* had been through.

That was bad enough, but then he dropped out. This was a habit. He'd gone to junior college to play basketball and then enrolled at California State University, Northridge, but didn't stay.

Now he didn't even want to finish his hours to get his license from beauty school. All he had left was basketball. Every day, he would just play pickup basketball games at a court in Burbank, right around the Disney studios. Not for money, mind you. There was no hustling in the least. It was just one endless loop of pickup games. His ambition didn't match mine, and as I completely supported him, I began to resent the other costs I was paying for being in an interracial relationship. We got snickers and stares everywhere we went, and his parents had wanted nothing to do with me until they saw the depth of his emotion when I was raped. It just wasn't worth it if I couldn't respect him.

I bought the *Waiting to Exhale* soundtrack just before I drove home to Pleasanton for Christmas break. I listened to it all the way there and all the way back. There are five stages of grieving love, and they are all there in that soundtrack: denial, anger, bargaining, depression, and acceptance. I resolved to end things with Alex through listening to those songs, but I didn't know how I was supposed to leave someone who was so absolutely dependent on me.

In Pleasanton I ran into Keith, who had been a senior at a nearby high school back when I was a freshman. Home for Christmas, we met up at a bar in Old Town Pleasanton. He was a star soccer player who got a scholarship to UCSB, and now he was in law school in San Diego. We hit it off and exchanged information. And we kept talking. He was very much like me if I hadn't had those Omaha summers to undo parts of my assimilation. He was so terminally corny.

I fell in Deep Like with Keith and began lying to Alex about reasons to go to San Diego. On the drives, I listened to my angst soundtrack of Whitney Houston, Chaka Khan, and Toni Braxton. As Toni sang "Let It Flow," I liked the idea of Keith even more. There was never an "Oh my God I want to fuck you" moment. But when you are young you start thinking that if you want to be a grown-up, you need a résumé guy. Someone who looks good on paper. Keith could be that guy for me.

My plan was to become brazen enough about Keith that Alex would break up with me. It's a trick I learned from my dad: you create a bad enough situation that the other half of the partnership just wants out. After all, Alex had always said, "If I ever find out that you're cheating, I'm just gonna leave."

One day I was driving down Wilshire in Westwood, just leaving the UCLA campus in my little Miata. My pager went off—call me Grandma and I'll kill you, but this is how we texted in the olden days. It was Alex.

"911," it read, which is how we kids expressed "Call me back now!" Then the numbers "04," which, upside down, spell out "ho."

"Oh," I said when I read "ho." I pulled into a 76 gas station on Wilshire and went to a pay phone.

"Get. Home. Now" was all Alex said.

I am not joking: My heart was dancing. He knew something and had called me a ho. The nuclear option was in play and I didn't have to do a thing. I listened to Whitney's "Exhale (Shoop Shoop)" on repeat the whole drive on the 405, joy filling me as I practiced my sad face. "Oh my God," I rehearsed in a flat, dull voice. "I can't believe this."

Alex was waiting with an envelope in his hand, addressed to me from Keith. I had two realizations. First, Alex had opened my mail, which just seemed rude. Second, corny Keith had sent a fucking love letter to my house. Just call me, dude.

"Here," Alex said, handing me the letter.

I took my time, reader. I took my sweet damn time wading through that boring-ass letter, and on page 2, I finally got to the portion of the program that sparked this scene.

"I've just got to say," Keith wrote, "the fellatio this weekend was very good."

I nodded a double confirmation—one for Alex now knowing I was cheating and one for Keith being corny enough to say "fellatio." I will say, however, that wanting to be caught cheating is different from having the specifics in print. So I just put on my game face.

"What is that?" Alex said, in a dramatic tearing-me-apart voice.

I paused. "It is what it is."

Nailed it! You know when you say shit and you think, Oooh, that was good. I was really impressed with myself.

Alex was just incredulous and looked like he was about to cry.

"Did you suck his dick, Nick?"

Look, I don't know if it was the Seussian title of *Did You Suck His Dick, Nick?* or the stress of the situation, but I just fell out into a lean-on-a-chair fit of laugh-crying.

"I did!" More laughter. "I did! What more proof do you need? Yes, 'fellatio.' I did."

This had to be it, right? It was over now.

Nope.

"I can't live without you," he said. "We can work this out."

Record scratch.

"You said you would leave if I cheated," I said, holding back what I wanted to say: "A deal is a fucking deal. Get OUT."

He started singing "Nobody Knows" by the Tony Rich Project. "Why didn't I say the things I needed to say? How could I let my angel get away . . . ?"

"You need your space to heal," I yelled, cutting him off before the chorus. "I don't deserve you. Go!"

Alex left, and then everything went radio silent. I'd gotten what I wanted, shoop shoop. But then I was stuck with Keith. He came to Black Graduation at UCLA, officially called the Afrikan Graduation Ceremony since its start in 1979. In front of all my cool friends, he gave me a crystal vase as a present. He was suddenly Grandpa to them. They were all taking pictures with it, putting the vase on their heads, pretending to drink booze from it. Then he corrected my grammar. Like the time I said "I think it would be funner to just do that."

"Funner? Is that a word?" he said. "Did you just make that up?"

So that ended that, just about the time I found out that Alex had fucked one of my best friends and was also dating a model and a Janet Jackson dancer. I was stuck with Crystal Vase Grammar Cop, and he had upgraded to a backup dancer? Hell, no. What if Alex was the one and I screwed it up because I was chasing a cornball? What if nobody ever loves me again?

So I became obsessed with what he was doing. Everything he was doing. I went back to the grief side of *Exhale,* with only Whitney's halting breathy voice to help. "Yes, why *does* it hurt . . . so bad, Whitney?"

If you're in the crazy-hurt passage of heartbreak, let's go on this ride together, shall we? One night I decided it made perfect sense to put on all-black clothing and a black knit cap and borrow my friend's car. I drove to Alex's apartment, where he now lived with his old college teammate. I closed the car door softly and skulked my skully-hatted ass into his bushes so I could look in his window. I just wanted to see his face. I wanted to know who he was with. This seemed perfectly rational.

There were no lights on, so when I got to the window, I could see myself reflected in the glass. I looked at my eyes, shining brightly at me.

"You are officially the psycho bitch," I said.

I'm not supposed to be in the bushes looking in someone's window. So I slowly, ever so slowly, crept back to the car like a hapless cat burglar coming up empty-handed.

I could have avoided all this if I just watched Angela Bassett in *Waiting to Exhale*. Angela plays Bernadine, who sets her husband's car ablaze, lamenting all the times she put him first, making herself the background to his foreground. She didn't pay for his beauty school, but she did become his secretary. It's the scene that created the term "Angela Bassett moment," an epic declaration of self-worth that I wanted for my mother and for everyone who realizes they got played. As I watch, I start screaming, and I can do every word. "But the worst, oh the fucking worst," she says, ripping his clothes out of his closet, only to later light the cigarette that will set them and his car ablaze. "The worst thing is that he made me move out here where my children are in school with only one other black kid so they won't be improperly influenced. Well, guess what, John? *You're* the motherfucking improper influence! Get your shit, get your shit, and get out!"

It's the moment where you reclaim your sanity by going insane, the burst of clarity that comes with blind rage. So, let Angela have it for you, breathe in the smoke from the car, and move on with her out of the bushes. In retrospect, I can say to myself, "Are you kidding me? Why would you lose it over that freaking loser?" But I know it doesn't ever feel like that in the moment. It feels reasonable to be in all black wearing a skully as you crouch in someone's bushes. Absolutely fucking reasonable.

PRO TIP: GIVE YOURSELF THE FULL TINA TURNER EXPERIENCE

What's Love Got to Do With It is, of course, based on Tina Turner's memoir, *I, Tina*. After my Greek-Mexican beauty school dropout, I went into full Tina immersion. I watched the movie, I read the book, and I had *that* film's soundtrack on repeat. If she'd put out a Tina Crunch cereal, I would have had it every morning.

I prescribe the Tina combo when you just want the pain to be over. You are about done with the nutty, even though it was supposed to be over months ago, and your instinct for independence needs a shot in the arm. Watch Angela Bassett play Tina finding that fire within her to go from her lowest to being Tina freaking Turner. She tells a divorce judge that she doesn't need anything else but freedom and her name. "I'll give up all that other stuff, but only if I get to keep my name," she says defiantly. "I've worked too hard for it, Your Honor."

Cut to me watching it for the fifteenth time, screaming, "Goddammit, give me my name! I just want my name." When I had my divorce, I went back and watched Tina. I still had my name.

I'm making a lot of jokes to cheer you up, but take this seriously: If you are feeling humiliated and broken by the weight of pain over someone trifling, be Tina. Let yourself be forged in this fire. I, for one, started my adolescence wanting to be Molly Ringwald, but I spent my twenties wanting to be Tina Turner.

As for that craziness I felt, one day I woke up and I just didn't feel it anymore. It left. It took time, but it left. It was as if the crazy was a gas bubble. You're just really uncomfortable and the very core of your body, your stomach and chest, hurts. And then you fart or drop a deuce and the pain leaves you. I promise you, it gets better. You will fart your way to healing, I swear.

PRO TIP: CUSHION THE BLOW WITH SOMEONE ELSE'S BODY

It's always beneficial in a breakup to have somebody else lined up. I really like to move right in and have a Plan B, C, D, and E in place before Plan A has expired.

As you go about this, your best game is honesty. Tell Plan B exactly where your head is at. "Do you want to be here? Yea or nay?" I don't even say, "This is a rebound." Don't even put that much weight on it. It's just fun. Tell them it's like hooking up with someone on vacation. Staycation sex.

It's on them if they think they can change the situation between you to create a lasting arrangement. Let them try, but at least you were very clear about your motivation from the start.

As you refocus your energy on someone else's privates, you save yourself the drudgery of going over in your mind what went wrong. Bitch, you know what went wrong. Unless this is your first guy, you're not that clueless. By your early to mid-twenties, you've been through this a few times, so you gotta know there's a common denominator in these equations—and it's *you*. I, like many women, know what the hell is wrong with me. Whether we choose to do something about it remains to be seen.

I know a lot of people talk about closure, "giving yourself time to mourn." Ehhh. Let's not play these games. I think the whole "pussy moratorium" thing is just some puritanical garbage to keep women chaste. I see it all the time in Hollywood. After the end of a relationship, an actress or famous woman has to publicly announce that her legs will be closed until further notice. Like some exorcist has to come in to flush out the demons from her vagina. Potential suitors, please wait until the little old lady from *Poltergeist* comes out and says, "THIS HOUSE IS CLEAN!"

You will hear, "You really need to work on yourself before you jump right into something else." Oh, please, who's got that kind of time? I got shit to do. I'm trying to work, I'm trying to get home to watch *Scandal,* and I'm trying to get it in. I could get hit by a bus tomorrow, and here I am using this time to work on myself.

By the way, you can work on yourself and still have sex with someone at the same time. Or at least *around* the same time. Your pussy and brain don't have to take turns. Besides, there's a bunch of hours in the day. You can actually get to therapy and go on a date on the same day.

Bonus Pro-tip: Booze Pairings to Heal Heartache

I will keep this short in case you are already reading this book at a bar. There are only two options for drinking your pain away after a breakup: red wine or tequila. Never mix, never worry.

Choose red wine if you'd like a warm hug and maybe a nap. A Malbec is that slightly bitter pal who rallies to say, "There, there, we'll get through this." A Cabernet is a model of efficiency, drinkable with a high alcohol content. With all of its varied flavors, Pinot is the one who'll encourage you to keep a sense of mystery.

But if you want to skip all that and just get to the point where you fuck one of his friends? You go tequila all the way. I prescribe straight, no chaser.

Either way, first round is on me.

twelve

ON MEAN WOMEN AND GOOD DOGS

One morning in early 2012, I got a call from *Essence* magazine. They wanted to give me the Fierce and Fearless award at their pre-Oscar luncheon in February. I had to give a speech, which I figured would last about thirty seconds. "Thank you," I'd say. "Yay, women."

Then they said I would have five minutes.

Whoa, I thought.

"If you give us your speech we can have it printed," they offered. That made it real. My instinct to protect myself shot up, and I immediately went to standard Hollywood cliché bullshit.

I started writing my speech on my laptop, saving the draft as a file titled "Fierce and Fearless." For days I would just look at the words on my computer screen. How was I supposed to be either of those things? I kept asking myself. I was so afraid that if I told the truth I would face judgment and rejection.

"We live in a town that rewards pretending," I typed. "And I had been pretending to be fierce and fearless for a very long time. I was a victim masquerading as a survivor."

I went to delete those lines, but kept going. "I used to revel in gossip and rumors. And I lived for the negativity inflicted upon my sister actresses or anyone I felt whose shine diminished my own. I took joy in people's pain and I tap-danced on their misery."

It was the most honest I'd ever been in my life. When the day came, I put on the armor of a green vintage Versace above-the-knee dress, and I took a deep breath as I approached the podium.

As I spoke, I felt the room become still. The murmur of chatter and ding of forks against plates stopped as I read my truth. People began to put arms around each other's shoulders, drawing them closer and crying. I stammered just slightly at one point, and I felt a wave of love come at me. These incredible, fierce women were all listening, pulling for me. Oprah Winfrey was there, her mouth wide open. Her seatmate Iyanla Vanzant reached over to close her mouth for her. "I had never heard anyone be that honest in public or private," Oprah said, "about the competition and fierce drive to be seen and succeed in Hollywood."

To be seen.

Leave it to Oprah to get to the heart of the matter. I was desperate just to be seen. I was afraid of anybody else getting attention. Because there's only so much to go around. With Oprah's benediction, people started acting like I was the Messiah and I would lead Hollywood's actresses to the promised land of mutual love. I wasn't ready. "I'm still in my own shit," I said.

And I really was. I had only recently found the courage to get up on that dais and be honest. I had been hiding, sometimes literally. I am someone who physically hides when I am feeling, let's say, stressed in a situation. Behind a garbage can, behind a tree. If I am somewhere and get an attack of the feels, I look for the nearest place to stash myself. I am the Where's Waldo? of emotional availability.

There was a particular moment in my life when I found myself hiding under my bed. I was in my early thirties and my life was a disappointment. My divorce was final, and I decided my career was over because a show I had a lot of hopes for was canceled. I slipped off my bed, looked underneath, and thought, Well, that looks cozy. So I scooted myself in, intending to stay there, oh, I don't know, forever.

My dog Bubba Sparxxx came into the bedroom to investigate my disappearance.

Bubba was a huge dog, about 130 pounds of Mastiff–American bulldog mix, but he was determined to do a marine crawl under that bed to get to me. His path to me was precise, like a longtime soldier carrying out a mission. We did have history. We had found each other in the middle of the night while I was shooting *Cradle 2 the Grave* at Los Alamitos Army Base, near Long Beach, California. It was a night shoot, and at 2 A.M., my costar DMX decided he wanted to buy some dogs. He needed a litter of dogs brought to the set right then. People just stood there, dumbfounded. I said, "I think I can help you."

So I called my then-husband Chris, who knew a guy who bred Royal Bandogs, mastiffs bred specifically with American bulldogs. So Chris called the breeder and this man showed up to the set at 3:45 A.M. with laundry baskets full of puppies. There were probably five or six dogs in total, all of them brown except one little white one. They were all so cute, and DMX picked out two, quickly naming them Pebbles and Bam Bam.

"You can take one of the dogs, too," the breeder said to me. "You got me the sale."

They were all adorable, but the little white one with a few brown spots seemed to call to me. I picked him up, round and white like a seal, and looked in his little amber eyes.

"Aw, you have an outie," I said, rubbing his little stomach.

"That's actually a hernia," said the breeder. "He's the runt. The hernia will either retract as he grows or he'll need surgery."

We needed each other.

"He's the one," I said. I named him Bubba Sparxxx after the white country-rapper, and he became my soul mate and best friend. He could tell when I came home frustrated. He'd stay very chill and wait for me to come around, without being pushy or needy. If I had big news, he was hyped about it before I even had a chance to articulate it to him. Whenever I had parties and he had the sense that some plus-one might be the least bit shady, he wouldn't let them walk around the house. Bubba never growled at anyone who wasn't foul.

He was just super intuitive. Which is how he knew to be under the bed. This huge lug of a dog crawled under the bed to look me in the eye. We regarded each other for a long time.

"Is this what we're doing today?" he said with his eyes. "Okay. It's cool, I just want to know. 'Cause I'm under here."

When I didn't respond, he began to lick my face. It was one of those moments where you just realize, Well, this is the most pathetic scene ever.

"Bubba," I said, "I think this is what the lady was talking about."

The lady was a trainer and life coach who had been hounding me at events. I had literally run from her at red carpets. It was like she could see through the façade. "When you're ready, call me," she'd say, pointing at me like a black female Tony Robbins. "You've got my number. You'll know when you're ready."

I reached up to get my cell from the bed. I had put her in my phone as Coach.

"Gabrielle," she answered, like she'd been waiting.

"I think this is what you were talking about when you said I'd know when I was ready."

WE MET IN A GYM ON A RAINY NOVEMBER DAY. SHE IMMEDIATELY PUT BOX-ing gloves on me. I started punching the heavy bag, going strong to impress her.

"What's on your Happy List?" Coach asked.

"My what?"

"You gotta do a Happy List," she said. "Tell me the things that make you happy."

I stalled, hitting harder. She asked me again, pointedly this time. Like a drill sergeant. "What makes you happy?"

I had nothing. I couldn't think of a single thing or single recent time I'd even been happy. Right away, I felt like I was failing a test. I started to cry, and my heart raced as my anxiety kicked in. I couldn't even do this right. My arms started to get numb from punching, so I slowed down.

"Come on," she yelled. "Give me three things and I'll let you stop punching the bag."

I kept punching, finally saying through gritted teeth, "Real butter."

Punch.

"Ground beef."

Punch. What else? Punch.

"Imitation crab," I said.

Punch.

I stopped, exhausted. Coach was looking at me with a mix of disgust and concern.

"Bitch," she said, "did you say imitation crab?"

In my mind, it was the best parts of the crab but so much less expensive.

"You don't even love the real thing?" she asked. "Can we just start there? The fact that they're all food items, we'll get to that later. Let's stop here, because there's so much more that we gotta get to before we can even think about nutrition."

She gave me the homework of writing down ten things that made me happy. We agreed to meet twice a week.

I went home and I couldn't get past the three. Real butter, ground beef, and imitation crab meat. I went back to her with the same three things the following week.

She shook her head at me again, and that session we didn't work out at all. We just sat in the gym and she threw out questions, dissecting the smallest pleasures of life.

"Do you like sunsets?" she asked. "Do you like sunrises?"

Even that made me cry. I didn't know.

"Um, uh," I ugly-cried. "Sunsets."

"Do you like crushed ice?" she asked. "Whole cubes?"

I panicked again, weighing the merits of both. "Um, when there's a bowl of ice . . ." I paused. I had something. "I like really, really cold Coronas."

"That's five," she shouted. She was the Annie Sullivan to my Helen Keller, helping me make sense of my world. I couldn't think of any more.

"You can't even think of ten things that make you happy," she said. "What made you think you were ready for marriage? How is someone else supposed to make you happy if *you* don't even know what makes you happy?"

We started in November, and by January I had finally found my ten things. Bubba was on the list. Before that, I couldn't say he made me happy because he was such a good dog I didn't think I deserved him. Coach and I started examining that kind of thinking, too, and started unraveling my life decisions from there.

One night I took Coach along with me to a party. By then I was less guarded with her and feeling bold. We were in a room at the party and I started holding court, using my well-honed ability to turn a phrase to tear down an actress who wasn't present. It was well honed because I used to feel I had to do it for survival, but now it was like I was killing for sport. As I ripped this absent woman to shreds, I felt like I was being fed as these people laughed and looked at me with faces that said, "More, more."

When I was done, there was nothing left of my target.

"How did that change your life?" Coach asked me after my performance.

"Excuse me?"

"Did you get her guy?" she asked. "Did you get her job? Is your house bigger now?"

I looked down at the ground, completely called out.

"What positive happened in your life because you tore this woman down?" she asked. "And, by the way, you showed exactly how much power she has over you because you spent an hour talking about her to a roomful of people."

I realized what I had been doing. When you're in a place where you don't know what makes you happy, it's really easy to be an asshole. I put other people's pain on my Happy List.

I went home that night, and sure enough, my house was not bigger for tearing that woman down. Bubba came to greet me and we sat in the living room.

"I'm trying, Bubba," I said. "You weren't always perfect, either."

Bubba was in fact a terror until he was two and a half, a whirling dervish of energy. My husband and I were with him in the park when we realized we needed to have him trained. A little boy was calling to him, so Bubba ran down an incline at full speed. His legs got away from him and he rolled into the kid like a bowling ball. The kid's mom thought it was funny, thank God, but then, as the boy was on the ground, Bubba sniffed him and then peed on him.

The first time we worked with a dog trainer, he bit the trainer. Which was a blessing, because that led me to trainers at a ranch that bills itself as the Disneyland of dog parks. They helped Bubba become the best dog in the history of dogs.

He changed. So could I.

AFTER MY *ESSENCE* SPEECH, THE MEDIA LATCHED ON TO THE MEAN-GIRL narrative of what I was saying. They missed the point, because it's not like I was some kid slamming people into lockers or spreading rumors about a sophomore. I was talking about being a woman. It's not like you age out of bullshit. It just sort of shape-shifts.

Because I was a mean woman, I can spot them. Game recognizes game, right? You encounter them every day if you work with other people, period. Whether you're a teacher, a lawyer in a large firm, or a stay-at-home mom. There is an epidemic now of people "being real" when they're being anything but. It's the person who loves being "someone" who notices every little thing wrong with what you say, do, wear, or think, and has to point it out. Those mean women, and mean men, affect people's opportunities and experiences, at work or with their children.

When I see negative comments about me online, if I have time I will go down the rabbit hole of social media to see how great the life of the troll really is. Because you never know, maybe they're right. Maybe they have something to teach me or for me to aspire to. I've done it countless times, Instastalking, Twitter stalking. Never once have I learned something from someone who talked shit. If anything, it's "Baby, you really don't want to put a bull's-eye on your back." But so many people really love the attention they get by trolling. It's a temporary cure for their invisibility.

The problem is, there's always an audience for negativity. There could be someone with a bullhorn screaming, "I've got a beautiful script here that gives a deeper insight into the human experience." And few in a crowd would pause. And then someone says "I've got Jennifer Lawrence's nudes," and a line will form. Negativity and the exploitation of other people's pain drive so much of our culture and conversation.

I know that, but I can still get caught up in my feelings. Recently I had an absolute complete meltdown over something said about me online. It was a castoff of a line, a joke the woman posted to get "oh the shade" likes and eyeballs. But I became fixated on it, imagining what I would say to her if she said it to my face, and knowing she never ever would.

I was with a friend when I saw it and held up my phone for her to see the post. I was full of "get this bitch" bravado, but she took my forearm and gently lowered it. Looking me in the eye, she said: "An empress does not concern herself with the antics of fools."

She smiled, so I smiled. That kindness, one empress to another, one woman to another, released me from the bullshit.

BUBBA DESERVES A CODA, BECAUSE HE'S THE ONE WHO GOT ME HERE. HE remained a good judge of character to the end. When Dwyane first came around, Bubba was apprehensive. One day, two full years into our relationship, the three of us were in the park and Bubba jumped up on the table where D was sitting. Bubba looked D in the eye, just like he'd done to me that morning under the bed. Then Bubba leaned in to nuzzle him. He was saying, "I like this guy."

From where I'm writing this, I can see Bubba's giant paw print in plaster. Yes, I really am that dog person. When he was twelve, he was given a year to live. By the grace of modern medicine and my pocketbook, we were able to keep him alive until he was thirteen. At one point we were thinking about getting him a new kidney. You had to agree to adopt the kidney-donor dog and commit to flying your sick dog up to UC Davis. Like I said, I'm that dog person. But we decided Bubba was old and it would all be too much to put two dogs through. When he finally passed, my whole circle went into mourning. If you knew Bubba, you loved Bubba.

When I call upon my ancestors and people who've passed to get me through something, I talk to him, too.

He saw me at my worst and my meanest, and he loved me anyway.

thirteen

WARNING: FAMOUS VAGINAS GET ITCHY, TOO

Dwyane and I are alone in the car outside the Walgreens in Miami.

"Just go in there," I say.

"Nope."

"You know what I use," I say. "You're in and out."

"You do it."

The subject is, of course, tampons, which I do not want to buy. Whenever I am in the feminine care section of any pharmacy, no matter how incognito I go, it's like an alert goes out. "Attention customers, Gabrielle Union has her period. Go say hi!"

Because if he goes in, yeah, he gets swarmed, but the response is "What a catch! He buys his wife tampons!" If I go in, whether it's a light day or it seems like I've been shot in my vagina, that intimate knowledge is sought out. Having knowledge about someone tending to her vagina is like sneaking a *Playboy*. "I saw Gabrielle Union buying *tampons*!" I'm a bleeding spectacle.

So you can imagine how unprepared I was when I suspected I had a yeast infection. 'Cause you know how loaded that is. Women aren't allowed to just get yeast infections as, say, part of the body's natural defense mechanism. We have to have caused it in some way—by wearing our underwear too tight, not changing our tampons often enough. Men can have jock itch for days and never once have to explain why.

I felt the first twinge while I was on a late-night flight to visit a guy I was dating before I married D. Let's call him Bachelor 1. B1 was extremely hung, and at the time he was sharing a beach house with his huge penis in Miami. The plan was that I would get to his place Friday night and he would arrive the next morning. This is also a guy who didn't believe women pooped, so a "Hey, shucks, I have a yeast infection" conversation was out of the question.

"Get thee to a CVS," I told myself upon landing.

It was about 1:00 A.M. by the time I stashed my bags at his place and set out for the 24-7 drugstore on Miami Beach. Here's what's great about a pharmacy by the beach in the middle of the night: nothing. It is teeming. Full. You think you are going to find it hopping with horny teens buying condoms, but it's a drunk in every aisle, white boys trying to figure out which cold medicines will make them higher, and, here and there, a crying girl hobbling along on one heel, looking for flip-flops. And in this particular outpost, one Gabrielle Union, trying to score some Monistat under cover of night.

I marched in, determined to be a grown woman seeing to her

over-the-counter vaginal cream needs. I was about three steps in when, I swear, every head in the place turned. My eyes darted to a display by the register.

"Twizzlers!" I said, striding over and picking up that bag like it was just the thing I was after and I couldn't believe my luck.

The guy at the register was a heavyset twenty-something who the managers probably thought looked intimidating enough to work the night shift. "Just these Twizzlers," I said, scanning the candy display in case I had any other last-minute sugar needs.

"Are you . . ." he said.

"Yes," I said. "How are *you*?"

"Do you want a bag?"

"No," I said. "I'm good."

Back in my car, I called a girlfriend on the West Coast. She always had an answer for everything. "Listen, I need to figure out a home remedy for a yeast infection."

"Cranberry juice," she said, not missing a beat. Dr. Quinn, Beverly Hills Medicine Woman. "Like, a boatload."

"On it," I replied. I waltzed right back into that CVS, waving hi to my register friend, as I pointed to the refrigerated section as if I had suddenly become parched. There were fifteen-ounce and sixty-four-ounce bottles of Cran-Apple, which I thought of as Regular and Maximum Strength. "Go big or go home," I said to myself, grabbing the sixty-four with one hand.

"Thirsty," I said to my register friend.

I drove back to B1's house, guzzling the cranberry juice the whole way. I still felt that now familiar and becoming-more-intense-by-the-minute burning, so I called my Dr. Quinn again.

"911, what's your emergency?" she said.

"When will it work?" I asked.

"You got a low-sugar one, right?"

"I got Cran-Apple."

"Gab, that's pure sugar. It will only make it worse!"

"Why didn't you tell me?" I yelled. "I just drank a half gallon of the shit." Malpractice!

"I think we need to try yogurt," she said. "You got to get some yogurt up in there. It will help."

"Stay with me," I said. I ran to B1's fridge and scanned the paltry bachelor contents.

"Okay!" I yelled, grabbing a Dannon vanilla. The flower of the vanilla plant beckoned me back to feminine health. "Doctor, I'll call you back," I said.

I wiggled out of my jeans and laid paper towels on the kitchen floor. Here goes nothing, I thought. I did my best, slathering the cold yogurt all around my vagina, but I couldn't quite get it inside to where the action needed to be.

Still lying on the floor, I reached again for the phone.

"I can't get it in," I nearly screamed. "It's too thick." The irony of saying this in the home of big-dicked B1 was not lost on me.

"You can't, like, spoon it in there?"

"No," I said. "And I can't make a syringe out of a ballpoint pen. I'm not freaking MacGyver."

She paused, as if she were consulting her witchy book of spells. "You need to make a tampon kind of thing," she said. "Suck the yogurt into a straw, insert it in like a tampon, and you can squeeze the yogurt up in there."

I went through every drawer in the kitchen. "What grown-up keeps straws?" I asked.

"I don't know your life," she said.

"You now know more than most."

"Well, go get one," she said. "A big, wide one. Like the ones at McDonald's."

I now took my yogurt-covered vagina to the McDonald's by the Delano that was open all night. Inside, there was a long line of the drunk people who weren't at CVS, the ones who had consumed enough alcohol at 2:30 A.M. to give up on their diets and give in to their cravings for French fries. The Girl Scout in me felt like I had to wait in line and at least buy a drink, but soon enough people started to recognize me.

So I jumped off the line and went right to the straw dispenser. I ripped the paper off and held it to my eye like a pirate with a telescope. "That should do it," I said aloud turning to see an employee stopping the work of sweeping to stare at me.

"Hi," I said, a little too loudly, grabbing a second one to ensure the sterility of this new medical tool. "You have a nice night."

While driving, I tried to calm my frayed nerves by imagining what that woman would tell her friends the next day. "Gabrielle Union was in here high as a kite looking for a coke straw!" Miraculously, this line of thinking did little to calm my frayed nerves.

Back at B1's, I learned that sucking yogurt through a straw is a little tougher than you'd think. But I did it. And once again I lay on the floor to squeeze the yogurt in. Whether it was psychosomatic or just psycho, I immediately felt like it was working. I hit redial.

"Is this the Dannon help line?" I asked.

"Dannon?" she said. "I hope you used plain."

"Shit, he only had vanilla."

"Christ," she said, laughing, "what is wrong with you?"

"That," I said, peering down at my yogurt vagina, "is a very fair question."

The absurdity of the whole night washed over me and I finally laughed. I was so scared of being judged for being a woman with a yeast infection that I was willing to put myself through any number of humiliations. I waltzed into a CVS, twice, and never left with what I needed. I stole a straw from McDonald's in the middle of the night! All to avoid my register friend knowing. I resolved that that would be the last night I found myself lying on some guy's kitchen floor shoving yogurt up my hoohah. I would live a more authentic life.

To a point. B1 rolled up the next morning, and he greeted me with a kiss.

"I ate your yogurt," I blurted out, trying very hard to seem not at all suspicious.

"Okaaaay," he said.

"I ate it," I said. "Just ate it."

He looked at me like I was crazy. Which I was. I mean, what else does one do with yogurt?

fourteen

GROWN-ASS-WOMAN BLUES

We are the ladies who lunch.

I have two girlfriends around my age, Michelle and Gwen, who I meet every few months or so for lunch when I am in Los Angeles. We are grown-ass women, and we are the only ones who understand each other's grown-ass problems.

"I apologize in advance for looking like a robot," I said when I came to the table at our last gathering. "I threw my neck out dancing."

"How?" asked Gwen.

"I tried to whip my hair back."

You see? Grown-ass problems.

"At least you're having fun," Michelle said, with Gwen silently nodding. They are both single, Gwen newly so after a twelve-year marriage. Michelle is awesome, but she never found anyone. That's the word she uses: "Anyone." Not even "the right guy." She is fun, and smart, and pretty, and she told me she feels invisible when she goes out. She sees what happens to the women her age who fight against invisibility to try to stand out. The ones who raid their daughters' closets or the ones who try so hard to lead a boisterous *Real Housewives* camera-ready life with a steady supply of booze. They at least draw attention, if fleeting, but Michelle doesn't want that. She's stuck, because if she does what comes natural to her and keeps it low key, guys won't even notice her. But if she shows she wants a relationship, men will flee.

"I have to act like I don't want it," she told me, "and then act surprised when it doesn't happen."

Meanwhile, Gwen is hot as hell and knows it. She got out of her marriage and went right to the bars. But that doesn't mean the puzzle isn't complicated for her as well.

"The men our age won't look at me," she said. "And I'm this weird science experiment for younger guys, chasing older pussy."

Single or partnered, successful or striving, we grown-ass women of the world share the feeling that we're all in an experiment that no one is particularly interested in watching except us. I see us all grasping at the straws of staying present in our lives and families and careers. Who knows how we will fare? I can only speak to my experience, so that is what I will do. To wit: Can an actress age in Hollywood and continue to work? All previous research has shown the answer to be a hearty NO, but it seems for my peers that so far, we are working way more than then we did in our twenties. But it's the opposite for my nonactor friends as they get older. Their competition for new jobs is younger people who make less and don't have families that they have to take off for. Oh shit, they say, we're those people that *we* pushed out. Women are told to "lean in." Yeah, right. "Lean in so I can push you over."

At lunch, Michelle told us about "the new black" at her company. "She's young and dope," she said. "And she's talking to me about dating. I'm like, 'Fuck you and your dating problems. You're me twenty years ago when I used to get dick.'"

We all nodded, except me, on account of my neck. I kind of moved forward.

"I have no patience for her," she said.

"That's because even though there are all these things that are supposed to be marked against her," said Gwen, "her skin color, the fact that she's a woman—none of that matters next to the fact that you're older. She gets your spot."

"Yeah," I said, swiveling my whole body to look at Michelle, "but who better to help her navigate that than you?"

"I'm not training the competition to do my job," said Michelle. "Would you?"

Um, no. And I thought about my own hypocrisy: Just the night before I had attended a pre-Oscar cocktail party for women in film. There I had met a young actor named Ryan Destiny. She had appeared in the Lee Daniels series *Star*. I had heard that she looked like me. I saw her in person and she looks like I literally gave birth to her. Gab 2.0, only better.

"Oh my God," she said. "I am finally meeting you. This is so amazing."

"What are you, twelve?"

"Twenty-two."

"Shit."

"I admire you so much," she said. "If you could mentor me . . ."

Bitch, fuck you, I thought. You want me to mentor you? The press is literally calling you the next Gabrielle Union . . . "except she can sing and dance!"

I smiled, and the photographers came over. They needed to document this moment of "Look who's old!" And I get it, because I have a reputation for never aging. And God, do I love that rep. But as the flashbulbs went off, I was suddenly terrified that the ruse would be up. Dorian Gray, turning to dust as she is photographed next to someone called the next Gabrielle Union.

Looking at Michelle and Gwen, I remembered not just the fear of suddenly looking decrepit next to this young woman, but the wave of panic that if I imparted my knowledge, I would lose in some kind of way. Would I be aiding and abetting myself into forced retirement and exile by helping this drop-dead gorgeous woman? A better, hotter, more talented version of me twenty-five years ago?

To be the women my friends and I are supposed to be, we are supposed to support the women coming up behind us. It's just hard to do that happily when you're finally at the table, and you feel any moment someone's going to come up, tap your shoulder, and say, "I think you're in my seat." It took me a long time to get that seat, goddammit. I'm not ready to move over just yet.

This fear resonates through every industry. For my friends in corporate America there's a reasonable fear about "mentoring" young women to be their best selves if that means they could take your job. Younger women are literally dangled in front of their older peers as a you-better-act-right stick to keep older, more experienced women in line. Because we've all seen a pal replaced for a younger, cheaper model with lower expectations and more free time for overtime or courting clients. Modern business is set up to squeeze out women who "want it all"—which is mostly just code for demanding equal pay for equal work. But the more empowered women in the workforce, the better. The more that women mentor women, the stronger our answer is to the old-boys' network that we've been left out of. We can't afford to leave any woman behind. We need every woman on the front lines lifting each other up . . . for the good of all of us and the women who come behind us.

It's tough to get past my own fears, so I have to remind myself that this is an experiment, to boldly go where no grown-ass woman has gone before. When we refuse to be exiled to the shadows as we mature, we get to be leaders who choose how we treat other women. If I don't support and mentor someone like Ryan, that's working from a place of fear. And if I put my foot on a rising star, that's perpetuating a cycle that will keep us all weak. The actresses in the generation before mine were well aware of their expiration dates, and they furiously tried to beat the clock before Hollywood had decided their milk had gone bad. Yes, there were some supremely catty women in Hollywood who actively spread rumors about younger stars so that they could stay working longer. But there were also way more amazing women who thought big picture. They trusted that if they uplifted each other, in twenty years, there might just be more work to go around. Women like Regina King, Tichina Arnold, Tisha Campbell-Martin, and Jenifer Lewis went out of their way to mentor and educate the next generation. That empowerment is why we have Taraji P. Henson, Kerry Washington, Viola Davis, Sanaa Lathan, and more starring in TV shows and producing films. That creates yet *more* work for the next woman up. That's what can happen when we mentor and empower. That's what happens when we realize that any joy we find in the next woman's pain or struggle is just a reflection of our own pain: "See how hard this is? Do you appreciate how difficult this is?" Instead, I want to heal her and me.

Christ. First a stiff neck and then I have to have this moral code? Nobody said being a grown-ass woman was easy.

fifteen

GET OUT OF MY PUSSY

I decided to finally go get this persistent pain in my hip checked. And my doctor in Miami, who happens to be a friend's dad and one of the world's leading neurosurgeons, told me to go for an MRI and X-ray at the hospital. Coincidentally, another fake round of "Gab's Knocked Up!" stories was making the rounds at exactly the same time. The photo evidence was that I'd worn a coat. In Toronto. At night. In winter. For sure, knocked up.

So here I am, walking into a hospital—right in the heart of Miami-Dade County—and everyone's clocking me. By the time I get to the imaging center, I've run through a gauntlet of knowing glances and "I see you" smiles. I know exactly what all these strangers are thinking. And there, as I am filling out the forms, is the question: "Are you pregnant?" I check "No."

"Head to room two and wait," says the lady behind the desk.

I go in, disrobe, put on the tissue-paper-thin gown, and sit on the table, tapping my feet on the step.

You know how, when you're in the doctor's office, each time the door opens, you think, This is it! and you raise your head expectantly, with a half smile that says, "I can make pleasantries but I will also take your role seriously"? This happens a couple of times.

The first time, there's a knock on the door and a nurse walks in. "I just want to double-check," she says, studying me. "We ask all women this: Are you pregnant?"

"Nope, it was on the form. I marked no."

"Okay. I just wanted to make sure."

Not a minute goes by before a different woman pops her head in.

"Yeah, okay. So, just want to make *sure,*" she says, drawing out "sure" as she looks me up and down. "Um, you've got no hairpins in your hair, no metal on. Your earrings are out?"

"Yes."

"Are you pregnant?"

"Nope. Not pregnant. Put it on the form."

"Well, hey, yeah, just making sure."

Finally, the X-ray tech arrives, and my hip and I are ready for our MRI close-up.

Ah, but my uterus is not done stealing the show. Because two *more* women walk in. How many damn people work here?

"Just want to make sure . . ." says the tall one. "You're not pregnant?"

Now I am just sad.

"No."

The shorter woman pats my leg in a rocking, petting motion.

"I just want to make sure you're not pregnant," she chimes in. "Because we really need to know. Because—"

Then I am angry.

"NOPE. NOT PREGNANT," I say, loudly, my heart beating fast and my arms becoming numb from anger.

"I filled out the form. You're now the fourth person to ask me. I am *not* pregnant. I know what the Web sites say. I'm telling you I'm not pregnant. If I was, I wouldn't fucking be here."

They quickly leave. And I lie there, thinking about how some Internet clickbait affected my medical care, thinking about what they will say about that girl Gabrielle Union, who came into the office today and is actually such a bitch.

When it is over, I do my best not to look at anyone. I keep my head down and put my sunglasses on as protection. I am almost to the door of the waiting room when another patient looks up from her magazine. She smiles and I smile back.

"You and Wade," she says, "would have such pretty babies."

I am out of the office before the tears come.

YES, DWYANE AND I WOULD HAVE SUCH PRETTY BABIES. BUT I HAVE HAD eight or nine miscarriages. In order to tell you the exact number, I would have to get out my medical records. (I am also not sure what the number is where you start to think I must be nuts to keep trying.)

I never wanted children before Dwyane. I was afraid to be attached to a man for life if our relationship didn't work out. After D got custody of the three children we raise, I was bursting with joy at every milestone—every basket scored and tough homework assignment completed. I was fulfilled raising children, a joy I never saw coming. Wanting to have babies with

Dwyane was a natural desire built on that joy. Dwyane wanted children with me for a long time before I was fully on board. For me, it was just a maybe, but one day we were with a friend's daughter and she smiled at me. My ovaries literally hurt. And I knew it was time.

For three years, my body has been a prisoner of trying to get pregnant—either been about to go into an IVF cycle, in the middle of an IVF cycle, or coming out of an IVF cycle. I have endured eight failed IVF cycles, with my body constantly full of hormones, and as you've probably figured out by now, yes, I am constantly bloated from these hormones. (It also means I have forgotten my normal baseline emotional reaction to any given situation, and have no idea whether it would resemble my I'm-going-to-hop-off-the-roof reaction.)

For as long as I can remember now, Dwyane and I have lived in this state of extended expectation. Did it take? Is the embryo normal or abnormal? Will I stay pregnant? We are always in some stage, waiting for some news, some sign that we can move on to the next stage. This child we want to have has been loved even as an idea. Each attempt at IVF is a loving action. So we remain here, bursting with love and ready to do anything to meet the child we've both dreamed of.

Many of our friends have had their marriages end with the stress that comes with fertility issues and the accompanying feelings of insecurity and failure, not to mention the testing and retesting, defining and redefining, of your identity as a woman. And this whole deal has wreaked havoc on my social life. I now hate going to baby showers, but the invitations are *constant*. I find myself making up excuses to avoid them. I hate hanging out with mothers who constantly talk about their kids—and what mother doesn't love to talk about her kids? (Well, actually, I do have some mom friends who can't stand their kids most of the time. Them, I like!)

People who know about my fertility issues often hand their babies to me to hold, or text me pictures of babies ("to keep your hope alive!" they say). Nobody seems to think that's insensitive, or maybe hard for me. So, no, I will not look at your Instagram if it's full of babies. Though D and I did enjoy the video a friend sent of her toddler sitting on the toilet and taking a crap—her face wrinkling with effort, then suddenly melting into surprise and relief. Comic gold! We watched it seventy-six times.

I did force myself to go to one baby shower recently, because I knew the woman had struggled with IVF. I wanted a winner's insight. I wanted to know what had pushed her to the finish line. "I sat my ass down," she said. "I quit my job and I stayed home and sat my ass down. That's all I focused on. That's all I did."

"That's all?" I wanted to say. "You gave up the work that you love?"

That's all.

Unfortunately, I kind of function as a single-income household. I may not support the family I've created with D, but I have several households of various family members I am alone responsible for. People assume I have a rich husband who pays for everything, practically giving me a salary. I don't, and I don't want that. So not working is simply not an option for me. And I know it's not an option for many women who want an opportunity to be a parent. It's awesome if that works in your life, and many people have assumed I can go this route, but the bank is weird about wanting their money. Those mortgages don't pay themselves. Maybe not asking my rich husband to pay all my bills makes me selfish and not mother material. But if I did that, I'd already feel like I failed as a mother.

DURING ANOTHER RECENT PREGNANCY RUMOR, I HAD TO DO A PRESS line, which is what you see when a celebrity is talking to a bunch of reporters at an event. *Ocean Drive,* a Miami-based magazine, was having a big party celebrating my being on their cover. I was happy to do it because I liked the article and the accompanying pictures. At the event, the editor of the magazine comes up.

"Oh my God, I loved #periodwatch," he says. It was the hashtag I created for my bloating.

I laugh. "Thanks."

He looks down. "I see you have a crop-top on tonight."

"This is my 'I swear to you, I am not pregnant' outfit," I joke.

It works. Reporters can tell I am not pregnant. Habeas corpus. Present the body. But it allows for a different question instead, posed by a gaggle of perfectly nice-looking people holding iPhones and tape recorders to my face: "Do you guys want to have kids?"

To avoid getting angry, I pivot toward what I think is a joke. "Have you ever asked my husband that question? Or any man?" Crickets. So I keep going. "'What's happening in your uterus?' 'How do you balance it all?'" hypothetical Reporter Me asks Celebrity Me. I pause, less joking now, my brittle anger just peeking through. "Until you ask my husband those same questions, I just can't answer them anymore."

But I can't stop. I can't help myself.

"Do you know why no one asks men how they balance it all? It's because there is no expectation of that. Bringing home money is enough. We don't expect you to be anything more than a provider, men. But a working woman? Not only do you have to bring home the bacon and fry it up, you gotta be a size double-zero, too. You've got to volunteer at the school, you've got to be a sex kitten, a great friend, a community activist. There are all these expectations that we put on women that we don't put on men. In the same way, we never inquire about what's happening in a man's urethra. 'Low sperm count, huh? That why you don't have kids? Have you tried IVF?'"

I have no takers on my rant. I am off the script and there is no editor alive who will use those lines in a caption or post about "Gabrielle's Baby Dreams." It reminds me of the time I did another press line with an actress who happened to know one of the reporters pretty well.

"How do you stay in such great shape?" asked the reporter.

"You know I don't eat," cracked my actress friend.

"No, I need something I can use," said the reporter.

"Oh." The actress thought for a second. "I eat broiled salmon and chicken with a lot of steamed veggies. After a while, you just really crave healthy food."

There you go: There's a script. You follow it. I mean, can you imagine if I said I didn't want kids? Say I answered "Do you and Dwyane want kids?" with "No." A woman in the public eye who doesn't want kids? She-devil. You probably kick puppies. And if you say, "Yes, I would like to have kids," they ask, "When are you starting? Have you had trouble? Are you facing infertility? What's wrong with your uterus? Do you have vaginal issues?" Wanting and not having opens you to all these rude, insensitive, prying questions that people ask. And if you do a full open kimono and say, "Here's the deal. I am doing IVF," the questions just get more personal, deeper. "Are you pregnant this week? This month? How did this cycle work out?" "Is your estrogen rising?" "How can I watch you on *Being Mary Jane* if I don't know the plans you have for your uterus?"

It's as if the whole world has a form, and they just really, really need to know if I am pregnant.

I want to scream, "Get out of my pussy! Just. Get. The. Fuck. Out."

That's the real story. Gabrielle Union's Baby Hopes: "Everyone Needs to Get Out of My Pussy!"

sixteen

AND GABRIELLE UNION AS . . . THE STEPMOTHER

My husband Dwyane has three sons, and in our home we are raising his two older sons, Zion, nine, and Zaire, fifteen, and also Dwyane's sixteen-year-old nephew, Dahveon, whom we call Dada. I am freakishly devoted to these boys. Zion is a fourth-grade genius and a born entertainer. He's me after a couple of drinks, making smart-ass comments and entertaining people. Dada and Zaire are both freshmen and girl crazy. Dada is Mr. Cool, letting friends seek him out, while Zaire is hyperconscious of the people around him. He is receptive to kindness and he is the one who will call you out if you're dismissive. He is desperate to make us proud, and one of my jobs as a stepmother is to remind him how smart and amazing he is. These boys are totally worthy of all the devotion I can offer.

When I first met the boys, I just wanted to be authentic. "I'm a cool motherfucker," I said to myself, checking my teeth in the mirror in the minutes before the introduction. "People like me." It was like we were all on a blind date. "Where are you from? What are your hobbies? What are your favorite movies?" And on we went.

As our relationship grew, I was determined to never try to be BFFs with the boys. I did my best to be a cool, reasonable, consistent adult. That's my advice to you stepparents out there. Whatever it is that you are, just be consistent. You can't be the cool permissive hippie one day and the disciplinarian the next. And to all current or potential stepmothers: unless the mother is dead or in jail—and even then—it's just a mistake to even try to scoot into her place. No one wants their mother replaced, whether she's Mother Teresa or a serial killer.

The boys were in on it when Dwyane proposed to me in December 2013. We all went to brunch in Miami and then the guys told me they wanted to go on a tour of our new house, which was still under construction. I say under construction, but it was more like a few pieces of wood and some nails.

"Are you gonna do your hair?" Dwyane asked me several times. "Are you gonna put on makeup?"

"To go to a construction site?" I asked. "No."

When we got there, the boys ran ahead of us to stand by what would eventually be our pool. "We want to do a presentation for you," said Zion. I thought they were going to do some kind of skit.

"Turn around," said Zaire.

So Dwyane and I faced away from the boys.

"Okay, we're ready," they said in unison.

The boys were all there with a sign. "Nickie, will you marry us?"

"Oh God, D," I said, thinking the boys were doing this on

their own. They had been after us to get married for two years. "This is awkward," I said, turning to Dwyane.

He was down on one knee with a ring.

"Will you marry us?"

"Oh," I said. "Oh. This is a thing. You guys are serious. Yes. Of course, yes!"

I love that they had agency in asking me to join the family. I never wanted to be the party crasher. The boys would have been especially vulnerable to someone trying to manipulate them because, as kids being raised by a male figure in a world that valorizes mothers as the sole models of nurturing, they all love the idea of "moms." If "traditional" moms had trading cards, they would have all of them. "The Cookie Baker." "The Classroom Volunteer." I don't fit into a traditional role, and I have too much respect for myself and these boys to attempt to fake it. They worship my mom, who they call Grammy, and my dad's wife, Nana to them. These women take being grandmothers very seriously, going to every school play and recital they can. They don't miss many.

But I do. A lot of events happen when I am literally out of state, at work. It doesn't matter why—all kids know is that you're missing it. It's even harder for D. He misses things because it's a game day, or he has practice. Even if he is in town, his work hours are not like anybody else's. He doesn't have the luxury of taking off early or having someone cover his shift. There are periods of time when neither of us is present, and this is not what either of us wants. As much as I try to be consistent, I'm often just absent. It's shockingly easy to parent by text or apps like Marco Polo or WhatsApp. But that feels lazy, and the whole time I'm using any of them I am thinking, I'm failing them. I'm failing them. I'm failing them.

I wish I had a job where the boys could see me leave for work in the morning and come home at night. They could watch me work on my lines and be a producer. I film *Being Mary Jane* in Atlanta, and I do movies wherever the good work is. I'm gone for a week, then swoop in for thirty-six hours of in-your-face time before flying out again. Even when I do get an extended break, they have the real lives of teenagers. They have family to visit and tournaments to play.

As I beat myself up about this, I realize that society does not provide great models of black women as nurturers of black children. Maybe as caregivers to white children, or the sassy, sage, asexual sidekick to a long-suffering white woman. Or maybe the "beat some sense into you" black mother we've seen in viral videos, but never as loving, kind, sensitive, or nurturing to black children. Recently our family was in our living room in our new house in Chicago. I was on the cream couch with my feet up on D's lap. He was just home from practice and telling a story about the ride home. It was a brutally cold day, about five degrees below zero, and his driver stopped at a light. They watched a woman get her toddler out of the car and put him out on the street while getting her stuff out of the trunk. The kid was basically standing in traffic, and without a coat. The light changed, but D's driver wouldn't go until the kid was safely out of the street. D nearly got out to help.

The woman then put on her own coat, finally took the child's hand, and proceeded to walk down the street still holding his coat. Now, I think we've all been with small children, and yes, getting them in and out of cars is a pain in the ass, but still. It was freezing—put the coat on the kid.

Zaire and Dada both said at the exact same time, "She was black, right?"

D paused. "Yeah."

The positive vision of motherhood, of nurturing love, is white. And I worry that my presence, flying in and flying out of their lives, is not offsetting the overriding schism between black womanhood and black motherhood. I can't catch up enough to undo the daily damage, and I hear that familiar mantra resounding in my head: I'm failing them, I'm failing them, I'm failing . . .

My very existence as a stepmother is a sign of failure and loss. Because, frankly, nobody likes the stepmother. The resounding message out there is "Bitch, sit down." I get that the idea of a stepmom is terrifying to a lot of biological moms. It can be hard to take the idea that somebody else is helping to raise your kids. Somebody else is at school on behalf of your kids.

"I didn't think *you'd* come," a teacher or administrator will always say when I go to the school. "What a *surprise*!" Part of that is that they see me in movies and on television. But I've also seen them do that to any woman with a job. Some of the other working moms and I formed an alliance at the boys' last school, but out of all the working moms I was the only stepparent. An understudy unfamiliar with the script, showing up and ad-libbing her ass off.

As a stepmother you have to remember your place. You play your position and stay in your lane. You don't overstep, and you're very aware that some people are waiting for that moment when you go too far. In interviews and even here in this book, I consciously refer to "our boys" or "the boys." You're not going to catch me saying, "my boys," and definitely not "my sons." I know how that would sound.

But any parent—step or otherwise—will go hard in the paint for the kids they love.

I am also very conscious that I am helping to raise young black men in a world where they are often in danger. I have watched them grow, and I have watched the world's perception of them change as they do. Zaire is now six foot one and Dada is five foot nine. They are not freakishly tall by the standards of their classmates, but after about nine years old, young black boys are suddenly perceived as young black men, and things start to change.

So, for their safety, I have taken to dropping these terrible Black Bombs on the boys. Black Bombs are what I call the inescapable truths of being a black person in this country, the things you do your children a disservice by not telling them about. I feel it is especially important that our boys, privileged black children in predominantly white, privileged neighborhoods, know these truths. Here they are living in luxury—and here I am to say, "Nuh-uh, homeboy. Plymouth Rock landed on *you*. Things aren't going to be the same for you." I tell them this when I see that they have their privilege blinders on.

The first time Zaire and Dada went to a sleepover, they were in sixth grade and we were still living in Miami. I drove them over to their friends' house, and they were opening the car doors before I even finished parking.

"Hold up!" I said. I turned to face them. They were sitting in the backseat, little duffel bags on their laps. "Do not wander around this house."

They looked at me dumbly.

"Only hang out where the family is."

"What?" asked Zaire.

"Because if something turns up missing, guess whose fault it is?"

Their faces were like cartoons—eyes wide, like, "Whaaaat?"

"They think I would steal?" asked Zaire.

"Yes. People think black people steal," I said. "Only hang out where other people are." Have fun at the sleepover, kids!

When they got older, I changed my script a bit. "Don't ever put yourself alone in a room with a white girl," I told them. "Or, in Miami, a Cuban girl."

They always gave me the same look: "Oh my God. Please stop talking."

"Her family is not happy about your little black dick," I said. "They're not happy about any of this." In the same way that we teach children not to run in the street, I need to teach them things to keep themselves alive. I have to tell them, "You talking back to a person of authority is not viewed in the same way as when your little white friend Eddie does it. People look at Eddie and say, 'Ah, here we have the makings of a leader! A free thinker to buck the system.'

"It doesn't matter who your parents are," I say. "You're going to be looked at as a thug or a problem child. Stand up for yourself? You're the bully."

I say to myself: "And the second you're not identified as Dwyane Wade's children, you are just young niggers."

At one of the boys' old schools, a dean said that Dada was bullying another black child. D was away, so I tagged in for the meeting. We had been through other incidents at this school. A boy playing basketball on the court one morning got frustrated when Zaire beat him. He called Zaire a nigger, and Dada jumped up to have his back. They didn't hit him, but this was still seen as poor behavior. Kids said "nigger" around the boys constantly, then blamed it on song lyrics. When I was in Pleasanton, the word simply wasn't as prevalent in music as it is now. There wasn't that handy excuse of singing it to a beat and saying, "Hey, it's the song." With me, it was a word the other kids had clearly heard at home.

"So I've taken the liberty of printing out spreadsheets for all of us," I said at the start of the meeting. "You can easily follow along on the agenda that we're going to cover today . . ."

This is actually not a joke. When I go to school meetings, I come with my books and articles to support what I'm talking about. Whether it's a Harvard study on implicit bias in academia or research into African American teenagers underperforming because they go to school with the burden of suspicion, I was ready to call them on their shit. That day I brought a copy of Ta-Nehisi Coates's *Between the World and Me.* Written as a letter to Coates's fifteen-year-old son, Samori, the book is a sort of guide to surviving in a black body in America.

"I think you should read it," I said, leaning forward to slide the book at the dean, "if you're interested in better reaching the black children whose parents pay tens of thousands of dollars to attend this school.

"So," I said, "did you label the other kid who started this disagreement a bully, or just our kid?"

"I didn't say bullying."

"Well, actually, you did," I said, passing him another printout. "Here's an e-mail chain where you used this very word in describing the incident to our nanny. You think our nanny from Wisconsin can't forward an e-mail?"

I explained the danger authority figures put black kids in when labeling them bullies. And I noted that they felt comfortable using that term because there was near-zero diversity in their faculty.

"What are you saying about black excellence or Latino excellence," I asked, "when the examples they see here are the crossing guard and the janitors? What message do you think that sends?"

It was just a fact that they disciplined others differently than our black boys. "How many times do our kids need to tell you that their classmates are using the word 'nigger'?" I asked. I had screen grabs of texts and e-mails where classmates used the word "nigger" and our kids told them to stop. "My kids have told you this," I said. "And what did you say?"

That had been dismissed as "typical boy behavior." Zaire was a bully. The administrators told me they hadn't thought of things that way. Cue the Oprah "aha" moment of nodding. It was revelation time. They didn't think of things that way because they'd never had to.

Here's the thing. I had to do all that—armed with spreadsheets and e-mails—to be taken seriously as a stepmother. At the end of the day, I could sign them out to take them to the dentist, but I didn't have the power to switch schools. That's D. That's the work of a *real* parent.

But guess what? We switched schools. The school officials could see it coming, and I could tell a stepmother's delivering the death blow made it especially painful.

OUR FRIEND PHIL BOUGHT A HOME IN OUR MIAMI NEIGHBORHOOD AND converted it into a basketball gym. Not just a court—we are talking Olympic-level training facilities. It's insane. I know this is some rich-people shit. When you see me owning the court on Snapchat? That's where I am. I should say this, too: Phil Collins bought J. Lo's house up the road from us. Different Phil. However, if I could get the drum crash from "In the Air Tonight" playing each time I sink a basket? Yes, please.

The gym is about eleven blocks away from our place and our friend Phil gave us a set of keys. "Anytime you want to stop by," he said, "let yourself in."

It was a Tuesday night in April when Zaire and Dada asked me if they could walk to the gym. It was 9 P.M. I was reading and didn't even look up.

"No, it's dark."

And that was that.

Cut to the next night: D was home from the playoffs, in a good mood, and they pulled the old okey-doke, like, "Let's get this sucker." I wasn't in the room.

This time it was 10 P.M., even later than when I said no. The boys were as sweet as could be. "Can we walk to Phil's gym?"

D said, "Sure. Here are my keys. I'm not sure if they work. I think he changed the locks. But try them." I now picture D in that moment, talking in a Jimmy Stewart voice: "Golly, guys! Try these keys repeatedly and see what happens!"

Then D casually came outside to join me on the dock. It was a beautiful night, a light wind coming off the water. Honeymoon weather.

"Hey, babe," I said.

"I told the boys they could go down to Phil's."

Record scratch.

"They just asked last night and I told them no. It's too dark."

"Well," he said, "I told them they could."

"D, it's too dark. People can't see them if they walk down North Bay."

"Babe, we've gotta cut the cord sometime."

I was already up, heart rate flying. North Bay is dark in some stretches, depending on how illuminated neighbors want their houses to be. You can be on a spotlit sidewalk one minute and "lurking" through trees the next.

"They're old enough," he said. "Think about what we were doing at their age." At their age I knew enough about the world to not trust that everything would be okay just because.

"This is an open-carry state, D," I reminded him, getting agitated. "A stand-your-ground state, and all our neighbors have to do to shoot these children is say they felt threatened. What's more threatening to our neighbors than two black boys 'lurking'? Walking down the street in front of their properties? We don't know half our neighbors. Half of them don't live here *half* the time. Do you trust these people to not kill our kids? Do you trust their security to not see our boys as threatening? If someone sees them, and the keys don't work . . . two black kids, D, two black kids."

D paused a moment, peering at me, turning the thought over in his head. "Let's go get 'em," he said. I had dropped another one of my Black Bombs, this time on him.

We literally hopped in the golf cart like *Mission: Impossible,* taking off down North Bay, D at the wheel, me dialing them on speaker.

Zaire answered on the third ring.

"Where are you?!"

"Um . . ."

"*That's* how I know you're fooling around," I yelled, the panic not quite yet unleashed but slowly working its way up my chest. "WHERE ARE YOU? Tell us specifically where you are."

"I think we're on Fifty-first Street. We're walking back. The keys didn't work."

I periscoped my head straight toward D, like, "I told you so."

As we drove our golf cart down the street, a cop car whooshed silently by. The thing about North Bay Road is that it's the most exclusive street in South Florida. A siren or flash of police lights would denote trouble, and if you're spending thirty million dollars on a mansion, you don't want to know there's trouble. That's why, in this neighborhood, police officers just roll up on you silently, like ninjas.

Then another one magically appeared. The squad car slowed down as it reached us, and the officer rolled down the window. Instinct kicked in. Dwyane and I froze.

"Oh," said the cop, genially. "Dwyane Wade."

"Hi," said D.

"Have a nice night," the cop said.

As he drove off, I stared straight ahead and gritted my teeth into a smile. "If you think these cops were not called on our boys, you are fucking delusional," I said.

These are privileged kids, I thought. Lord knows what they would say when the cops reached them. I would like to think they would be polite, but under duress, who knows. I realized it was completely possible they would say, "I *live* here, motherfucker."

Soon we found them on the side of the road, walking toward us. Before we did, I turned to D. His eyes were on the road.

"What did you tell the kids to say when they're stopped by police?" I asked him.

"Well, I told them what to say in case—"

"WHAT did you tell them?"

"I told them to say their full names and our address."

"Wrong answer," I say. "'I'm Dwyane Wade's kid.' *That's* what they say."

AS WE ZOOMED DOWN THE ROAD IN OUR STUPID GOLF CART LOOKING for the kids, my mind flashed back to March the year before. Zaire was in seventh grade and he'd asked if he could take our Dalmatian–pit bull mix, Pink, out for a walk with Dada. It was a negotiation.

"Okay, walk down to the Boshes'," we said. D's old Heat teammate Chris Bosh lived eleven doors down the road. I figured they could walk out the door and I would have our security call the Boshes' security to warn them.

As they bounded out, I stood at the door, ready to drop a Black Bomb. "Wrap the dog leash around your thumb," I said to them. "That way, your fingers are free to spread." This was an actual conversation I had. But this is what you did three years after Trayvon Martin and five months after Tamir Rice. I didn't want the boys to have their hands in their pockets or for them to look as if they were concealing something dangerous.

Zaire started to open his mouth, and I shut him down.

"You've gotta walk Pink that way," I said. "It's not just the police. It's the neighborhood security officers, too. Anyone who is armed can harm you."

Sure enough, the first time they walked Pink, it was a disaster. That was the night someone swatted Lil Wayne's house over on La Gorce Island, near us. Now, if you are a celebrity, swatting is a nightmare. Someone calls 911 as a prank, announces a hostage situation or shooting at a famous person's house, and watches the news as a SWAT team storms the mansion. It's happened to Justin Bieber, Miley Cyrus, Ashton Kutcher—any bored thirteen-year-old can make a call and then watch the show. It's happened to poor Lil Wayne twice.

So there were two boys walking a huge dog as a dozen police cars flew past them. At our house, our security guards started to go crazy, talking about a shooting. Chris's security then radioed in, practically yelling, "Abort mission!" about walking a dog. It was like an international incident.

As more and more cop cars raced by the kids, they froze on the side of the road. They assumed the cars were for them. "Oh my God," I imagined them saying to each other. "This is what she is always talking about!"

The last cop car stopped and rolled down the window, just like they had done with D and me in the golf cart. He was looking at our two black kids. He didn't say a word—just stared.

And what did Zaire do? That boy dropped the leash and ran. Dada followed. They just took off, with a pit-Dalmatian running after them like *Boyz in the Waterfront Community Hood.*

I had gone over this and over this with them, but when the shit hit the Shinola, they just didn't know what to do.

Zaire and Dada told us all the whole story that night in the kitchen. The boys were laughing now, the edges of the experience dulling into an anecdote. I'd poured a glass of Chardonnay to calm myself down. I swirled the wine in my mouth for a second as they talked excitedly, tasting the notes of pear and white chocolate with hints of vanilla. I was drinking wine and listening to what amounted to a boys' adventure story told in a million-dollar custom-made kitchen. None of it would protect us.

"They could have shot you in the back," I said.

BACK TO THE GOLF CART, SEARCHING FOR ZAIRE AND DADA, WHO WERE probably fumbling with their keys and looking to everyone else in the world like two black boys staging a break-in.

I felt mad at them, I felt mad at D, and I felt mad at how black boys seem to be in constant danger. (And these are not just black boys. These are *big* black boys, especially endangered.) How are we supposed to give them all the knowledge, all the power, and all the pride that we can, and then ask them to be subservient when it comes to dealing with the police? "This is how you have to act in order to come home alive."

They are the boys I adore. And people don't value their very breath. It could be extinguished in one second, without thought, leaving a dog to run, dragging its leash the whole way home. A dog, safer from harm than black boy bodies.

seventeen

MITTENS

When Dwyane moved back to Chicago to play for the Bulls, we began renting a Victorian-style house on the Gold Coast. The boy who grew up hearing shootings on the South Side of Chicago now lives in the most expensive neighborhood in the city. The house was built in 1883, and one of the first owners was successful adman Charles Kingsbury Miller, a Son of the American Revolution who proudly traced his lineage to colonial families. For his postretirement second act, he led the charge for legislation to make it illegal to disrespect the American flag. He was especially upset, he said in an 1898 SAR banquet speech, to see the flag "converted into grotesque coats for Negro minstrels." The home was recently restored to preserve its sense of history, so it is easy to imagine Charles returning to visit and the look on his face when he finds me at the door.

When I am in town, I leave the house every morning to walk to the gym. In the winter it is eight degrees in broad daylight, and everyone and their mother is wearing the uniform of a big black puffy coat with the hood up. You can see two inches of everyone's face. As I walk, I see my Gold Coast neighbors scan the visible slash of my skin. They're looking to see if I belong to one of the houses. Am I the cook? The nanny? Whose girl am I?

The sidewalks are narrow here because a lot of our neighbors have literally gated their shrubs. There's the shrubbery in front of their home, then the sidewalk, and then more fenced-in shrubbery before the street. Why they need to wall off their shrubbery is another topic for conversation, but the result is that if you stop to talk with somebody, you literally block the whole sidewalk.

Yesterday on my walk, two women did just that. One had a dog on a short leash and the other was an older woman I recognized as a close neighbor. As I approached them with their backs turned to me, I rehearsed what to say to avoid scaring them.

"Excuse me, ladies," I said in my sweetest, singsongiest voice. The older woman turned, reacting with a full face of pleasantness. But as she saw my two inches of skin, I watched a wave of terror come over her face as her entire body clenched.

I sidled past, and as I walked away, I heard my neighbor say something I couldn't place, but then heard the last word as clear as could be: "thug."

Was she talking about me? The kids? My sweet husband, who I often call Poopy? Something completely unrelated to me? Whatever the answer, I gave my workout to her. I thought about her saying "thug" the entire time I was on the treadmill, pounding out that run.

The next day, as I layered up to make my walk to the gym, I remembered that I had two new pairs of gloves and mittens, both in black and white stripes. I instinctively reached for the gloves, but I stopped.

"Well," I said aloud, "thugs don't wear mittens."

I put the mittens on and went out into the street. Of course I was fumbling with my phone because, honestly, you can't do shit with mittens on. But I was going to make my neighbors feel comfortable, dammit. Surely they would see my black face and say, "But wait, she's got on mittens! She's an acceptable Negro. She *belongs*. Just look at those darling mittens."

That day, I decided to walk through the park instead of on the sidewalk. To save myself two minutes, I cut from the path to walk across a patch of grass. I was four steps in when I got trapped in a quicksand of icy mud. I looked down, my sneakers getting muddier and muddier, and I wasn't sure where to step next.

Suddenly, a sea of children ran toward me. They were probably on a field trip, racing through the park, with their teachers trying to keep up. "What are the teachers going to think about this black lady," I thought to myself, "in a puffy coat and black hoodie, standing frozen in this swamp of mud?"

I panicked, sticking my hands out at my sides. I've got my mittens on, I thought. Those teachers can tell their children not to be afraid. As the kids ran around me, I tried to skedaddle past them, because that is the only word for the ridiculous "walking" I was doing, slipping and sliding across the icy mud. And I became furious. Had I really reassured myself that I could erase four hundred years of history with these fucking mittens? Yes, the mittens were the thing that was going to separate *me* from the other black people who my neighbors deem threatening or, at very least, have decided don't belong on the Gold Coast.

I had dared to go off the path set for me. But when I got to the gym, I didn't think about my neighbors on the treadmill that day. I thought about my friend Ricky Williams. Ricky is a retired Miami Dolphin who I met while I was doing *Bad Boys II*. He would be the first to tell you that he has social anxiety, so we bonded over that right away. I called him Buddha because he was so cosmic and sweet. Like me, he likes to go for walks, and like me, he doesn't always know where he's headed. When I'm filming in new cities, I walk around and allow myself to get lost. And yes, I have been known to aimlessly follow squirrels.

Ricky was showing just that trait in January 2017, before an award ceremony in Tyler, Texas, when this ex–University of Texas prodigal son left his hotel to kill time with a walk. Ricky was strolling through nearby woods when someone called the police because he looked "suspicious." On the body-cam footage, before the officers even got out of the car, one of them said, "That looks like Ricky Williams." It was actually four cops who arrived on "the scene" to search and question him. He was told to put his hands behind his back, and right after they told him to spread his legs, a starstruck young officer asked if he was Ricky Williams.

"I am."

What followed presents a surreal portrait of fame and the black body. On video, the cops seem to slip in and out of seeing him as Ricky Williams, someone whose fame sets him apart, and seeing a black man in a white space. Ricky stands there as the cop runs his hands all over his body. "I'll explain everything to you in just a second," says the cop, pulling Ricky's hotel key card from his pocket. "People don't know who you are, nothing may have happened that was wrong, but we gotta find out."

When Ricky tells them he is staying at the Marriott next door, the policemen seem to leap on this fact as a reason to let him go. "If you tell me you're staying at this hotel," says one officer, "it makes a little more sense as to why you're walking around this area."

Ricky then shows just the slightest crack in his Buddha cool, and points out that the cop had pulled out his hotel card.

"Isn't that the whole point of searching me?" asks Ricky. "To get information?"

"You're not in handcuffs. We're just talking to you."

"Why would I be in handcuffs? I didn't do anything wrong."

"You're acting really defensive."

And then Ricky tells the truth: "Do you know how many times I've been messed with by the cops because I'm black?"

"Oh, no no no no," says a cop, as the others shake their heads. "Come on now."

Yes, come on now. There was an assumption of guilt because of his very identity, and Ricky had to convince these men that he was innocent. The police stopped him as a reminder of the power structure Ricky is supposed to enforce upon himself: he should know that his skin puts him under constant surveillance and that his very presence outside of sanctioned spaces creates the assumption of wrongdoing. It is, in fact, an inconvenience to the police that they have to be bothered to tell him this. By now, as adults, Ricky and I are supposed to have internalized these rules and regulations that come with our very existence. We put on the mittens, we utter singsong hellos, and we stay where we belong.

I cut through the little field at the park that day. If someone had stopped me and I had to try to explain my moves, why I opted to go through the park, why I came across these children, why I was sliding through the mud . . . if I had tried to explain myself, I might have sounded crazy, but really all I would have been explaining away was the presence of my body in a space where it has been decided that black bodies are violent and threatening.

Worse, I am told that people don't want to hear these stories, but the reality is we experience life in a never-ending loop in which we are told that if we just "make it," we will enjoy the fruits of our labor: assimilation. My father tried so hard, but he was pulled out of his Mercedes at gunpoint in Pleasanton on his way to work in a suit. The police said they were looking for an escaped convict from nearby Santa Rita Jail. My father was a middle-aged man who looked nothing like the convict except for being black. There was no neighborhood outcry or protest. No one came to his defense. It was a necessary "inconvenience" for maintaining the safety of the neighborhood.

But what does that say about aspirational living? Hey, you moved into a big house and you made it . . . except you didn't. There's this idea that you will be safe if you just get famous enough, successful enough, pull yourself up by your bootstraps, move into the right neighborhood, do all these things to fully assimilate into the America people have been sold on. We all bought in, and we keep thinking if we just get over this mountain of assimilation, on the other side is a pot of gold. Or maybe a unicorn, perhaps a leprechaun. Any of those is as plausible as the acceptance of the wholeness of me. But there's just another mountain on the other side. And someone will be ready to tell you, "Don't be breathing hard. You need to make this look easy."

Just as the cops were annoyed when Ricky said he had been repeatedly stopped because he is black, discussion of race is often dismissed or talked over unless it is in a sanctioned space. You can talk about your experience at a roundtable on race, but don't talk about yourself at a "regular" roundtable. It is exactly the same as when I would challenge my friends in Pleasanton near the end of high school. "That again?" they would say. "Get off your soapbox." Only now these are grown-ups who fashion themselves as allies. But these are my stories; this is what I have lived. I know what the boys I raise go through, what my husband goes through, and beyond my family, I can watch a video of it happening to Ricky. Each of us experiences these "same things," but each experience has value and deserves telling. I need to write them and read them aloud to constantly remind myself of my reality. I need to hear these stories. If I think mittens—or the way I talk, or the fame I have—will make my breathing and living on this planet permissible.

I am told no one wants to hear about it. I even hear it from other people of color in Hollywood. Some have climbed the mountain and have been able to assimilate so thoroughly, they think they are in a parallel universe. "You're sabotaging your own success by limiting yourself to being a black woman," they say. They tell us that if we just stripped away these layers of identity, we would be perceived not for our color or gender, but for our inner core. Our "humanness."

My humanness doesn't insulate me from racism or sexism. In fact, I think I can deal effectively with the world precisely because I am a black woman who is so comfortable in my black-womanness. I know what I can accomplish. And anything I have accomplished, I did so not in spite of being a black woman, but *because* I am a black woman.

This is not the message that assimilated people of color in Hollywood want to hear. In exchange for a temporary pass that they think is permanent, these ones who've "made it" then turn and yell back to the others, "No, keep going! Assimilation is the key! Deny your victimhood! Let go of your identity."

Better bring your mittens, that's what I know.

eighteen

BIG BANK TAKE LITTLE BANK

Dwyane and I have a ritual involving our favorite show, *Nashville.* I guess I should say our favorite show that I am not on. No matter what, we have to watch it together, preferably at home in Chicago. We have these twin chaise lounges in our theater room, and in winter, we each have a blanket to curl up in, fuzzy on one side, quilted on the other.

We always assemble our snacks beforehand because we don't want to get up during the show. It's all about being able to barrel through the episode. Lately we've been doing Garrett's popcorn in the tubs, half cheese, half caramel corn. Then I have my alkaline water and he's got the bottled water he likes. And of course we have our phones beside us, too, so we can tweet about *Nashville*, which is almost as good as watching *Nashville*. We even have our own phone chargers ready—go big or go home.

If you don't watch the show, just understand that Deacon and

Rayna were everything. Through all their ups and downs, their love endured and we adored them for it. I'm writing this in a hotel in New York City, and D and I have signed in under the alias Deacon Claybourne. (I also check in stealth as Cha Cha diGregorio from *Grease*—the best dancer at St. Bernadette's with the worst reputation—but that is another story.)

Without giving anything away, one of Deacon and Rayna's issues as a couple in country music is that she is the huge singing star and earner in the relationship. When Deacon told Rayna, "It's your world, I just live in it," that was the most honest description I have heard about the inequity of fame and finances in love. I know it rang true for me. That's how all my relationships were before Dwyane. I paid for everything.

The first time my father ever met Dwyane, it was at Dad's house in Arizona. We successfully navigated the whole awkward first meeting, but at the very last second, just as we were leaving, Dad pulled Dwyane back into the house.

"What do you want with my daughter?" he asked, suddenly gruff. "She's got her own shit. She's got her own house. She's got her own money. What do you want with my daughter?"

He wasn't saying, "What are your intentions for my daughter's heart?" He meant, "We have been down this road before and she's come out poorer."

Dad didn't believe that a professional athlete wasn't hiding some problem that would prove a drain on my savings. "I'm doing all right by myself," D then awkwardly explained. "I'm not going to try to use her."

He doesn't need my money, but sometimes I'm Deacon and it really is Dwyane's world. I often work around his life, because I have more flexibility. Because the basketball schedule is the basketball schedule, amen. And, at the end of September, that schedule is our schedule. On top of that, he has many brand and partnership obligations. Then there are the team obligations, the NBA obligations, and in between that there's our family. And then there's us as a couple. A lot of times I am like, "Whatever, just tell me when I can see you."

We are lucky in that we have homes in many cities now, because we're all over the place for work, and that's where I can plainly see the lines of division. I make it clear to people that there is a house I am financially responsible for in L.A., and there is the Miami home Dwyane built when he played for the Heat. "Don't judge the black actress home that I pay for in Los Angeles," I say when folks visit. "I know you've seen the black athlete home in Miami, but this is what I can afford."

D thinks the disparity is funny, probably because he's loaded. There are times when we go to restaurants and D will purposefully forget his wallet so I have to pay. Once, at the end of a large, boozy gathering, I texted him under the guise of answering a question from my publicist. "I wouldn't have said, 'Let's invite your whole team out!' if I knew this was going on the black actress AmEx that you don't chip in for." He loved that one.

When we were designing the Miami home, my husband kept saying things like "Well, I didn't want to sign off on that until you saw it."

"At the end of the day it's your money," I would answer, "so do whatever you want to do."

"But you're the woman of the house," he'd say. "You're my partner, you're here with me."

That was lovely, but in all negotiations, whether it was about wallpaper or if we *really* needed to get an eight-foot-tall Buddha statue in the Miami house, I have learned this lesson: big bank take little bank.

It's a simple rule dictating that whoever has more money wins. Whatever your income bracket, whoever has the power of the bigger purse in the relationship usually has the final decision. In my first marriage, I made more than my husband, so I was big bank. Now, I was decidedly little bank. The sanctity of this rule was never more apparent than when we worked out the prenup. On paper, it's an adult thing to do. Grown-ups with a certain amount of money who care for each other say, "You know what, just in case we gotta jump ship, let's make clear while we really like each other exactly what we're going in with and what we leave with."

The negotiations went on for months before our August 2014 wedding. We started with the right intentions, mind you. My team and I were adamant that we have a prenup to protect myself, because I got taken to the cleaners in my first marriage. Dwyane's team was all in because he had been to the cleaners with his first wife. We both basically bought our respective cleaners, plus the deli next door, and built a new wing on the library across the street. That's how bad those divorces had been. It wasn't that either of us planned on getting divorced. But we also didn't plan on getting cleaned out again, either. Better safe than losing all your money, you know? My first thought was that I wanted to leave the marriage, should things go that way, with whatever I came in with. I wanted Dwyane to know I didn't need his *anything* if I didn't want to be with him. I will give blow jobs in a leper colony before I take a dime from a man I am no longer in love with. That's who I am. I will cut off my nose, or my lips I guess, to spite my face.

But Dwayne felt differently. His team kept pushing. "No, no.

We want to give you something, throw out some numbers." So finally, I gave in. It was like they said, "You can have whatever salad you want," and I asked for a kale salad.

"Actually," they replied with a note of apology, "it's just iceberg lettuce for you."

"But you said I could have whatever I wanted," I answered. "I want kale. Why would you offer me anything if you only wanted to give me iceberg? Don't you care about my health and wellness?"

This was all coming from Dwyane's team, yes, but the person who had proposed to me was now, in theory, lowballing me. It wasn't even about the money, really. The question for me was "What does this man think I'm worth?" There were literally pages going back and forth, detailing my potential worth as a wife. The money went up if I had a child, and then there were even weirder conversations about my own earning potential. When my attorney eventually had to say, "Fuck you, these are her quotes," meaning what I am paid to do a job, I realized we were negotiating my marriage the same way we would a sitcom deal at NBC. My team had to provide examples of my past worth, then factor in my social media power to come up with a number that I needed to protect as my future earnings. And then Dwyane's team came back with, "No, actually, that's not her value. She is worth less than that."

"Worth less." I tried that on in my actress voices. "I am worth less. Worth less? Worthless. Ah, yes, I am worthless." My number was based off my own work, whereas his angle was just "This is what I want to pay."

Big bank take little bank.

It was hell, especially when you're supposed to be marrying your best friend. Finally, three days before the wedding, he became Dwyane again. You know why? Because I signed. He was like Jon Snow, morphing from "Winter is coming" to "I'm in Miami, bitch!" He became ecstatic, throwing off all the layers of anxiety, and there I was underneath them, the woman he loved. He was freed. But I was resentful. Hell, I am still resentful. Which is why when I make him my #ManCrushMonday on Instagram, I say, "As per the prenup, my forever man crush Monday." Does he regret playing hardball? Not in the least. He played to win.

Thank God our wedding was fun. Honestly, our wedding saved our marriage. I fell in love with him five different times that night. When I say I had the time of my life, I really mean every word. After our reception, all the guests were given candles. And then a gospel choir led us in a march, singing "God Is Trying to Tell You Something" from *The Color Purple*. So we marched with our candles, and people shared wishes for us and wishes for themselves. The choir led us into a supersized 1930s juke joint we created just for the night. Questlove was DJing, and one of my favorite bands, Guy, was on the stage. We had a rocking chair rest area for the older folks, and we were surrounded by all of our favorite people—the people who valued us for our real worth. The best thing was that people danced all night. If you left the dance floor it was just to get more booze and then you went right back. It went on for hours, and Dwyane and I were the very last to leave.

I think about our vows sometimes. "If you've ever wondered if I'll leave you, the answer is never," Dwyane said to me in front of all those people. "And if you've ever wondered what I value, the answer is you."

I needed to hear that, and I needed to tell him what I said

in return. "This day is about the two of us coming together and being the best team possible," I said. "So today, I vow to love you without conditions." And I had to add one very important promise:

"I vow not to watch *Scandal* or *Nashville* without you."

Even under the rules of big bank take little bank, so far, so good.

nineteen

THE ROOM WHERE IT HAPPENS

The text came from a number I didn't know. Prince's invites would always be this way. Last minute and straightforward, with the address of a house he was renting in Los Angeles for awards season, or later, a hotel he was taking over for the night.

My first came in 2005. I grabbed my friend's hand and showed her the text. We were at a Grammy weekend party in L.A. and were having a great time, but this was a much better offer.

"We're going," I said. "Now."

The whole way to the mysterious address, I was sure the invitation was a prank. Maybe, I thought, it would be better that way. I was terrified of showing up at Prince's house and being lame. I was sure there were going to be way cooler people than me there, and I was going to be the idiot who said the wrong thing.

The house was at the end of a steep driveway up Mulholland, and my friend and I made our way to the door. I was still waiting for the "Oh, there must be a mistake." But the security guy gave me a nod. Then he looked at my friend.

"Did you get a text?" the large man asked, as politely as possible.

"No," she said.

"I'm sorry" was all he said.

Now, my friend is dope as hell and also happens to be someone famous. You know her, and if I told you her name you would immediately know that of course she could hang. But Prince planned his invite list like a precision instrument. And I had the golden ticket that night.

"You *have* to go in," she said.

"Okaythecarwilltakeyouhomeloveyou," I said, because there was no way I was *not* going in. And I felt lucky to have a friend who understood what this invitation meant.

The first thing I noticed as I walked through the door was that this was definitely Prince's house. Purple tapestries, music blasting, candles everywhere . . .

"Dearly beloved . . ." I said to myself.

To my right was a huge staircase, and to my left, just beyond the crowd, stood Whitney Houston, Mariah Carey, and Mary J. Blige in a small circle. They were still in their Grammy party gowns, looking like my nineties soulful-pop fantasies come to life.

"Oh my God, Gabrielle," Mary said, waving me over. "That picture we took at Quincy's party, I have it on my mantel. I see you every day."

"Really?" I asked, meaning it. Mary J. Blige had a picture of *me*?

"Come, come," she said, drawing me into their circle. I don't really get starstruck, but as I was doing air kisses with these icons,

I thought, How in the hell is this even happening? These gorgeous, important women were in the middle of having a legit kiki. I think that word gets overused, but this was a kiki of epic proportions. Mariah was sipping champagne and telling a story about some guy trying to come on to her. She is an amazing storyteller—deadpan, but landing the details about this chump perfectly as Whitney let out that amazing roar of a laugh of hers. It was like being invited to sit at the cool table. I had grown up watching all these women, dying to meet them, and here they were, having girl talk like at a slumber party with friends and inviting me in. Just some normal superstars, talking about life. Stars, They're Just Like Us, only not at all, because this was Prince's house.

I spotted our host across the room, sitting on the stairs and talking intently to Anthony Anderson. I later asked Anthony what they talked about.

"Jehovah," said Anthony.

Prince was, as he would say, living "in the truth." As a Jehovah's Witness rooted in his faith, he recognized that there were elements of his beliefs that could touch other people. You didn't have to buy the whole faith, lock, stock, and barrel. But there were aspects that he found comfort and guidance in that he wanted to share. As he talked to Anthony, Prince moved his head ever so slightly. Even his smallest movements were musical.

I was mesmerized watching him, and it took Matthew McConaughey to break the spell, running by with a set of bongos. "Wow," I thought, "that is a thing that guy actually does." Then I saw my friend Sanaa Lathan talking with Hill Harper. I spotted Damon Wayans making Renée Zellweger guffaw, and Salma Hayek dancing with Penélope Cruz.

Suddenly, Prince just appeared in front of me.

"Thank you so much for inviting me," I said. Oh God, I thought, what am I supposed to call him? "Mr. Prince."

He smiled. Stop! I screamed in my head. Shut up! I was petrified of saying something stupid. So I did.

"I feel like I should have brought a tuna casserole," I said. Fuck, you idiot.

He raised one magnificent, exquisitely sculpted eyebrow.

"We're both from the Midwest," I said, unable to stop myself from talking. "That's what we do, right?"

His face broke into a smile. "I love tuna casserole," he said, in his low, deliberate voice. "And I liked you on that episode of *ER*. I really liked it."

"How are you watching *ER*?" I said. "You're Prince."

"I see everything," he said.

And I believed him, looking around the room at a completely random collection of faces from music, television, and film. His parties also included writers, directors, and producers of all types of content. There was always a random athlete or two in the mix as well. It was all over the place, and completely inclusive at the same time. I'd never seen anything like it.

THERE WAS A REASON. HOLLYWOOD IS EXTREMELY SEGREGATED. THE whole idea of Black Hollywood, Latino Hollywood, Asian Hollywood—it's very real. And it all stems from who is with you in the audition rooms as you are coming up. Because you are generally auditioning with people who look like you, over and over again, simply because of how roles are described. When it got down to the wire for the role of "Sassy Friend #1," these were the people I saw. That's how I got to know Zoe Saldana, Kerry Washington, Essence Atkins, Robinne Lee, Sanaa, and all the Reginas. Sassy Friend #1 was a black girl between x and y age, and that meant a very shallow casting pool. When it came time to cast a family, I would meet an array of actors who all looked like me. Sitting in those rooms for hours at a time, multiple times a week, you get to know people.

As you all start to rise, it's the same people, who are now deemed the "it folk," who you sit in better rooms with. And those people become your community; they know the struggle you went through, because they went through it, too. And the rooms pretty much stay that way, no matter how high you rise, because for the most part Hollywood doesn't really subscribe to colorblind casting. What Lin-Manuel Miranda did with *Hamilton* is literally unheard of. We black actors meet in the room into which we are invited, but we are often barred from, to steal from Lin, *the room where it happens*. The spaces where deals get made and ideas get traded. Half the time you get picked to do something in Hollywood, it's because someone cosigned for you. "Oh yeah, she's talented, but more important, she's cool," someone with more pull than you will say. "I hung out with her this one time."

But how do you hang when you're not at the same parties? The biggest award show parties come with very rare invites, and the brown people you see there are the same brown people that have been starring in things forever. Unless you spend at least five grand a month on a power publicist to help land a spot, it's not gonna just "happen." Black actresses are rarely deemed the ingénues, or even the up-and-comers. So your work or even a spark of public interest isn't a guarantee. But let's say you make it into the room, whether through pay-to-play or luck. You're in. You got the golden ticket.

So, let's go in together. First off, the light is amazing, but you're too wired from the red carpet to do anything but rush to find the closest drink. These red-carpet appearances are timed to the second, so that there won't be a big collision of big stars. Performers are scheduled and served up like courses at a meal. If your entrance is set for eight thirty and your car gets there at eight? Circle the block, bitch, because someone more important than you has a better call time. And unfortunately, if you have a late call time, a lot of people will have left the party by the time you cross that threshold. That feeling though, when this wall of cameras fires at you and you hear the machine-gun rat-a-tat of clicks, is exhilarating. Your every move creates a new wave of shots.

Once inside, you're just another beautiful person in this beautifully lit room full of writers, producers, directors, and studio heads. Yes, this is a great chance to network and get to know people, but if you are one of only a sprinkling of black folks in the room, how does that even happen? Just because you're there doesn't mean anyone's gonna talk to you—trust me. No one has vouched for you in the way that Prince had. You feel like an interloper, and you go for the familiar. Because you know who is for sure going to talk with you? The other brown people.

Here's the thing about the #OscarsSoWhite discussion. Hollywood films are so white because their art happens in a vacuum. It is made by white filmmakers, with white actors, for imagined white audiences. No one even thinks of remedying the issue through communal partying. Inviting one black actor to the party isn't enough—sorry, folks. We all know you can create even better art by truly being inclusive, but you're never going to get inclusive in your work if you can't figure out how to get inclusive in your social life. If you're an actor of color and you've never had the chance to hang out with somebody and show them you're talented and fun and enlightened and deeper than what you can submit on a résumé, you never have the opportunities to be included. Prince created those opportunities just by throwing a better party. When he included you, you literally found yourself in the bathroom line with some of the world's biggest names in entertainment. How we gauge what success is supposed to look like is different for white actors than it is for black actors. And I am aware that half my résumé looks like crumbs to many white actors.

The films *Deliver Us from Eva* and *Two Can Play That Game*—these are hood classics, if not cult classics like *Bring It On*. A lot of people appreciate these films, but because there aren't any white people in them, they get marginalized and put on a separate shelf. They are underappreciated, but they never lost money. And I will continue to do these movies—ones I call FUBU, For Us by Us—because I love them and I am grateful for them.

I made lifelong friends on the sets of these films. The black Hollywood community is so small that we all came up together and created opportunities for each other. These movies set the stage for twenty-plus years of careers. It's a testament to the community that we, over the years, have always looked out for each other and pitched each other for jobs. I am incredibly grateful for that love we have for one another and the mutual respect of talent that we bring to the table. None of us benefit from tearing each other down. There aren't enough of us. We need each other to lean on.

Now, a lot of white people have been like, "I have loved you since *Bring It On*." But the ones who made sure I had a career were black people. White people will say, "Oh, Taraji just came on the scene with *Benjamin Button*, and now look at her on *Empire*!" The truth is, Taraji has been working for a thousand years.

White people just met Cookie, but black people have known and supported and *loved* Taraji forever.

I remember when Taraji got her first invite to one of Prince's parties. Prince was renting Cuttino Mobley's place and gave an outdoor concert. Taraji was pure joy, dancing and singing. Every single person at that party looked around and thought, "Why isn't it like this all the time?"

I WAS LUCKY TO GO TO ENOUGH OF PRINCE'S PARTIES THAT WE DEVEL-oped a friendship. By that I mean that I went from saying "Mr. Prince" to, at least, "Heeey, Prince." His gatherings were always held around some event or awards show I was going to, and the invites never came directly. One of the last times I saw him, he invited me to a small dinner party in Las Vegas. He was doing a residency at the Rio, and they had provided him with a palatial suite to use for his stay. In attendance that night were Ludacris, Hill Harper, Shaun Robinson, Dave Chappelle, Toni Braxton, Atlanta DJ Ryan Cameron, and me. I was sitting between Luda and Toni, and we were all starving, waiting for Prince to come in and take his seat at the head of the table.

Finally, he arrived and we were served a squash soup. Before we started, he asked us all to join hands in prayer.

"Dear Lord . . ." he said, pausing dramatically, "Jehovah."

Luda, Toni, and I squeezed each other's hands at that. Honestly, I don't remember any other food because I couldn't shut up about how good that soup was. But I remember the conversation. Again and again, over this epic three-hour dinner, Prince kept looping back to spirituality and social responsibility. Even when I told him how much I loved his parties, he explained there was a religious component.

"I want to understand people," he said, "to see what unites them."

He was also funny, repeating phrases he found comical, like "I'm not sayin', I'm just sayin'." Melodic punch lines, over and over, keeping us all laughing.

Then we went to watch him perform. It was after midnight by then, at a small venue so we could get up close. As his guests, we were closest to him, and it felt like as he improvised his set that night, he chose the songs based on the conversations we'd had at dinner. It was like the music was the soundtrack to *us*.

I OWE MY MARRIAGE TO PRINCE. THAT'S WHAT A CONNECTOR HE WAS. IN January 2007, Prince announced, with just a few hours' notice, that he was hosting a Golden Globes after-party on the rooftop of the Beverly Wilshire hotel. When the text arrived, I knew where I had to be. I was heading up in the elevator with Diddy—always Puff to me—and Nia Long, when Dwyane's brother Donny stepped on.

"Oh my God," said Donny. "My brother is your biggest fan."

"Who's your brother?" I asked.

"Dwyane Wade."

"No shit?" said Puffy.

"That's nice," I said.

"Listen," said Donny, almost at his floor. "We've been trying to get in touch with your people about cohosting a party with him for the Super Bowl in Miami. Would you be interested?"

I was already seeing someone in Miami and was head over heels for that guy, so I thought, Why not? I was not thinking of Dwyane as a love interest at all, and I didn't even meet him before the party. I brought Sanaa and Patti LaBelle. I was taking Miss

Patti to the bathroom and D happened to be standing at the top of the stairs.

"Oh, hey," I said. "I'm throwing this party with you."

"Hey," he said shyly.

"Um, we're gonna be over there if you wanna come join," I said. It was just courtesy. He seemed nice enough, but quiet. For me, there was no chemistry.

I didn't take D seriously until much later. He became a friend, and then he became my best friend. We were talking about something completely unrelated to us, and I looked at him and I just knew: I didn't want to be on this planet without him. I didn't want to not bear witness to him succeeding. I chose him.

When Prince died in 2016, Dwyane took his death hard. He hadn't spent any time with Prince, and frankly I was a little like, "Hey, there is a hierarchy of grief, you know . . ." Shortly after Prince died, someone got hold of an old, little-heard Australian radio interview with one of Prince's protégés, Damaris Lewis. She was ballsy, quite funny, and she bragged during the interview that she could call Prince and get him to talk. She did, and basketball came up.

"Well, Dwyane Wade is my favorite player," Prince had said.

Someone played it for D right before a game, and minutes later he teared up over it during the National Anthem. I know this message from Prince said to him, "I am on the right track." For me, it cosigned every wonderful thing I feel about Dwyane. We were both welcome at the party.

The world mourned an icon, playing "Purple Rain," a song I adore but I know he made thirty years before his passing. As tributes froze him in that amber, I noticed that stories of his parties started popping up on entertainment blogs. Whitewashed accounts of people begging Justin Timberlake to sing, with barely a mention of the black or brown guests at the parties. Either the authors didn't notice them, or they just didn't know our names.

I mourn the icon, too, but I grieve the vital connector who brought so many communities together, long after he recorded those radio hits everyone knows by heart. He gamed the system to provide access for talented people to access each other. Perhaps if he were white, he would be celebrated as a modern Warhol, famous not just for his own art, but for creating a space where interesting people with money and talent, or just one or the other, could meet and create. His own diverse Factory. Instead, the parties are reduced to jam sessions, just as the women he gave opportunities to—artists like Sheila E., Wendy & Lisa, Vanity, Apollonia, Chaka Khan, Susanna Hoffs, Rosie Gaines, Misty Copeland, Janelle Monáe, Damaris—are reduced to haremlike roundups. Prince's women. *I'm not saying, I'm just saying.*

I still wonder who could take up his mantle, and if it's even possible. Who could be cool enough to bring all these different, interesting people together in the name of art and communion?

I also have a selfish thought. In all the times I spent with Prince, I wish I'd just once had the balls to ask him, "What is it you see in me? That maybe I am not seeing in myself?"

twenty

A TALE OF TWO MARTINEZES

"Okay, pass your homework to the front."

I'm not going to say a wave of panic washed over me, but let's say it was a splash. I was five minutes into algebra class, the second day of my freshman year of high school. As the guy behind me tapped my shoulder with his paper, I raised my hand.

"I didn't know there was homework," I said, reaching back without looking. I had missed class the day before because there was a mix-up with my schedule. Besides, who gives homework the first day?

"Then you should have asked a friend, Nickie," Mr. Fuller said. I'd heard Fuller was a hard-ass, a Vietnam vet prone to outbursts.

"I didn't know who was in the class," I said.

"You don't have any friends?" he said. "Well, we need to fix that."

Fuller went to his desk and scrawled something on a sheet of paper before taping it to the wall. The sheet had FONU in huge letters.

"Who wants to join the Friends of Nickie Union club?" he said. "Now she'll know who to call the next time she blows off class."

For a long, long minute there was just a stunned tittering, and no one got up. Finally, the guy behind me walked over to the sheet and wrote his name. Ray Martinez. When he sat down, I turned to him.

He leaned in to whisper.

"Do you like Salt-N-Pepa? Have you heard 'Push It'?"

Cue the music. Ray Martinez was a sophomore who had just transferred with his little sister Kristen from somewhere in New Jersey. She was a year younger than me, and everyone called her Sookie. They were Puerto Rican, which people not so lovingly referred to as "Mexican."

Pretty soon after the FONU incident, Fuller took an extended sabbatical. The big rumor was that he'd had a Vietnam flashback and thought a kid was Vietcong. In any case, we had a slew of substitutes for the rest of the term. None of them were real algebra teachers, so the subs basically just gave everyone a passing grade no matter what. We had it made for the rest of the year.

Ray was on my track team, and he could already drive any car he could get his hands on. We'd hang out all the time, bonding over our love of dance music. He had a yellow Sony Walkman with him at all times, and we would listen to the TDK and Maxell tapes his cousins made for him off the radio in New York City. We didn't have BET, and MTV barely played black music by people whose last name wasn't Jackson, so these tapes were golden. The music of KISS-FM and WBLS, freestyle, house, and hip-hop, exuded so much emotion, and we were there for all of it. We started cutting class together, making a pilgrimage to Rasputin's, a record shop in Berkeley, to find dance singles. We'd return in time for track practice, having car-danced the whole way back.

Ray and Sookie's stepdad, Jim, had an old-fashioned Studebaker, and Ray figured out how to jump-start it without the key. Ray and Sookie would roll over in the Studebaker, playing his cousins' tapes, and we'd joyride around, transported to New York by the master-mixes of black and Latino DJs. One time we decided to write a rap song of our own. I say song, but it was just a bunch of dirty sexual lines with cuss words written on notebook paper. Ray put it in his pocket and Jim found it in the laundry. Jim declared me a bad influence and forbade me from ever seeing Ray and Sookie again. That lasted two hours.

Ray started hanging out with all my other girlfriends right away. In his Z. Cavaricci pants, Ray could blend in with the boys, but he took dance class. That was a tell for a lot of the adults around us, who could detect in him what we kids were oblivious to. When it came to Ray, all of our parents were . . . well, there is no nice way to say "homophobic." Not my mom, but certainly my dad. He and all the dads had nicknames for Ray. Sweet Ray, Sugar Ray, and one even referred to him as Ray-Gay. It's not surprising. These were the dads who drove us kids into San Francisco to go to Pier 39, saying, "You're listening to K-F-A-G San Francisco, rocking you from behind."

When everyone you meet says, "fag," it becomes part of your own language. I would use that word to describe a thousand and one things. Saying "You're a fag" was akin to saying "You're a dick." Like "nigger," it was just a negative word, used widely, and

I absolutely used it widely. Even growing up with my very nonhomophobic, openhearted mom, the pull of assimilation overshot my common sense.

One Christmas Eve, my sisters and I were listening to the cast recording of *Dreamgirls* and acting out all the parts. The doorbell rang, and it was Ray and Sookie. She was crying, and the side of Ray's face was swollen. He could barely open his eye. Their stepdad Jim's family was in town, and an extended family member had punched Ray in the face. My mom tended to Ray with ice in the kitchen, and Sookie just told me that the person had called Ray a bad name. Sookie was a year younger than me, but in that moment we formed a small bond that would flourish. I decided Sookie and I were Ray's protectors, even if I didn't know what I was protecting him from.

Ray and my mom returned to the living room and he just happened to know every word to Deena Jones's songs. Despite all the obvious signs, I still assumed Ray was straight, because that's what I thought he was supposed to be as a teenage boy in Pleasanton. He would also go to great lengths to pretend to have crushes on girls, and he even briefly had a girlfriend. There was also a beautiful girl in our class who was desperate to sleep with Ray—and my crew and I pressured him to fuck her. We just wanted him to get some action. We had this same conversation, over and over:

Me: You better fuck that girl.

Ray: I'm not ready.

Chorus: What the hell?!

Looking back, this is the worst-case scenario of peer pressure for a young gay man, and we just kept right on. At seventeen, we realized you only had to be eighteen to see the live sex shows in the Mission District in San Francisco. We were good bluffers, so we'd head into San Francisco and drag Ray with us, basically forcing him into these clubs. "This is how to be straight. Look, that guy likes it! You will, too."

WHEN I WAS A JUNIOR, RAY'S SISTER SOOKIE BECAME MY CUTTING BUDDY. We'd ditch school and go into Oakland, because we had both developed a deep and abiding love of black boys. Every weekend she and I would go to After Dark, an all-ages club twenty miles away in Walnut Creek. After Dark was like Disneyland for brown girls. Every time we went, we found something that never existed in Pleasanton—a whole room of boys who could like us.

We would be *so* pumped when it came time to go out, and put so much into coordinating our outfits. Our go-to look was slightly cropped long-sleeve sweaters with jean shorts and high-tech boots. My hair I modeled after Janet Jackson in the "Black Cat" video.

On the drive over to After Dark, we would always listen to a tape of L'Trimm singing "Cars That Go Boom" to psyche ourselves up. L'Trimm was a hip-hop duo of girls our age. They'd met in high school, just like us. After Dark was in an industrial park, and I remember the walk up to the door was everything. My heart would be thumping, and I would want so much to be a bad bitch and have every head turn when I went in.

The club felt physically big to me then, but it was just a medium-sized, one-story box. They didn't serve alcohol, but older guys would come with booze in their cars. They guys were in groups, separated by city and car. There were these Suzuki Samurai guys, each with a small towel draped across the shoulder, which I never understood. Then there were the 5.0 Mustang guys and the guys with the gold Dayton rims. Even their hubcaps had a message. And separately, there were the ones who always wore polka dots and had Gumby haircuts.

We collected boys' numbers, talking to them on the phone and then calling each other to deliver instant replays. My relationship with Sookie developed separately from my friendship with Ray. I had two best friends. Ray and I shared a hunger for the culture of music that I only heard when I would go back to Omaha. He represented that slice of heaven. He had bigger aspirations than living in a nice house in Pleasanton and maybe achieving membership in a country club. He wanted to travel the world.

With Sookie, I had a kindred spirit and a partner in crime—someone interested in the same type of guys as me. I never had to explain what I felt to her, she just got it. And like Ray, we shared a love of being anywhere but Pleasanton. Going to clubs with her, we met more and more people, and my world expanded beyond high school.

WHEN RAY GRADUATED, HE WORKED AT A MARIE CALLENDER'S RESTAUrant the summer before college. My girlfriends and I would go in for discounted meals and talk about where we'd go after. Ray was always talking about going to San Francisco, to this one place where he really loved the food. He said he'd get an omelet.

It just became a joke. "Oh, Ray's going to San Francisco for eggs." It never occurred to us—or it never occurred to me—that he was going to be with his community.

That was also the summer of "Ray's Fake ID." Ray and Sook had an older brother, Sam, who looked exactly like him, so he'd borrow his license. Anyone throwing a party knew to call Ray to get booze. It was always all love at the beginning of the party, but once people started drinking, the fag jokes would start.

"Sweet Ray, Ray-Gay . . ."

One time I was sitting on the curb at a party, wearing overalls and my high-tech boots. I was finishing off a forty of Mickey's big mouth, and some kids started in calling Ray a faggot. He didn't say a word, letting it pass. I began to see red.

I broke my forty on the curb and turned it toward the whole crowd.

"He's not a fucking faggot!" I screamed. "He is not a fucking faggot!"

I was threatening an entire party because I didn't want Ray to be other. I would have cut somebody. My friends grabbed me and drove away with me still screaming.

I wish I could say that I was protecting Ray. I was protecting me. I already felt like an outsider, and I had run a shell game on all these people to fit in. I could not allow people to point out another way in which someone close to me was "other." In trying to control the situation, I was unconsciously trying to control Ray.

I WENT TO THE UNIVERSITY OF NEBRASKA FOR MY FRESHMAN YEAR OF college. While I was home for Christmas break we all had a huge party at a girlfriend's house. We trashed the place, so when we woke up the next morning we set about cleaning up. I was in the living room doing as good a job with a broom as my hangover would allow. I noticed that everyone was acting cagey with me.

"What is going on?" I asked.

"Ray, just tell her," someone finally said. "Just tell her."

Ray sat me down on the couch.

"Nickie, I'm gay," he said.

"Really?" I started crying. "Who knows?"

"Everyone."

"Everyone?" I said. "Ray, *I* am your best friend."

Everyone knew but me. He was taking them to gay clubs and opening them up to new worlds. And nobody could have open conversations about this around me, least of all Ray. People just got sick of it.

He took a deep breath, and his tone became angry.

"Do you know how many times I have listened to you say 'faggot' or 'fag'? Now, think of all the times you've complained to me about people saying 'nigger' or talking shit about black people. You were so fucking comfortable using the same language, and you were too selfish to know you were hurting me. You were breaking my heart *every time*."

"I'm sorry," I said, bawling now.

"Yes, you are my best friend," he said, beginning to cry, too. "And I felt like I couldn't share it with you because you were so committed to being ignorant so you could fit in with these motherfuckers. Was it worth it, Nickie?"

I've never been more disappointed in myself. I'd humiliated myself with my ignorance, and in the process hurt one of the people closest to me. It was devastating.

Again and again, I told him I was sorry, and when he hugged me I melted into him on the couch.

"You know when would have been a good time to tell me you're gay?" I said. "That time when I took on the whole party, asshole."

We both burst out laughing. About the lengths I had gone to to protect my notion of his heterosexuality. I was too busy protecting our spots on a Jenga tower of assimilationist bullshit to be the friend he needed.

RAY STUDIED DANCE IN COLLEGE AND THEN GOT A JOB DOING ENTERTAINment on cruise ships. He was fully out by then, and he would send me letters from random places. Dusseldorf, Ibiza, Nicaragua. He was wild, living out the adolescence he didn't have in Pleasanton. When he talked about guys, my know-it-all controlling voice would kick in, lecturing him about safe sex. He told me he met a Canadian guy, and pretty soon he wanted to just settle down in one place with him. He moved to Santa Monica.

Sookie moved to New York to work for Urban Outfitters. My first-ever trip to New York was to visit her in her little walk-up in Park Slope, Brooklyn. I was twenty-two and got lost on the subway. I remember going into a bodega to ask for directions and thinking I was going to be shot.

Living on different coasts, Sook and I didn't see much of each other throughout our twenties, but when we did it was as best friends again. As my career took off, she and Ray would joke about knowing Nickie Union, not Gabrielle. They were very aware of the difference between Nickie and Gabrielle. They appreciated Nickie and went out of their way to say that was who they wanted to be friends with. They wanted to make sure I didn't get lost.

There was this magic time when Sookie and I literally ran into each other in Vegas. It was early 2006, and it was like seeing a mirage. Neither of us knew the other would be there, and we glommed onto each other for the whole night.

She had a secret. The year before, in July, she had felt a lump in her breast. She was thirty, had just started a new position at Urban, and was moving into a new apartment. She didn't want to admit she had a lump. She made a doctor's appointment for September, but when the doctor canceled it she never rescheduled. Life, as John Lennon said, is what happens when you're making other plans. It would be six months before she had a diagnosis: advanced metastatic breast cancer.

She made Ray call me because she couldn't talk about it. He was sobbing.

"Stage four?" I said. "Out of how many?"

"Four."

She was afraid to tell me, the same exact way Ray was afraid to tell me he was gay. And I was angry. "How dare you not prioritize yourself?" I wanted to yell at her. "Because now I am going to be without a friend. How dare you be so selfish?" We always internalize the things that happen to other people in terms of how it will affect us. I had literally just run into Sook in Vegas, and then she goes and gets cancer. I wanted to ask her how she had time to go to Vegas and didn't have time to go get that lump checked out?

As time marches on and you look back, you realize how easily this can happen. Like, "Oh, I've got this weird twinge in my thigh . . . but I gotta go to work." When you are busy, you don't think you have the luxury of taking time off to sit in a doctor's office.

We all do it. Nobody wants to even go to the emergency room with a cut. "Okay, I can't get the bleeding to stop. Fuck. I suppose I have to go." You knew five hours ago you needed stitches, but you were just hoping. In her case, it turned out to be stage IV metastatic cancer.

I didn't have that perspective at the time. I needed to be useful and control the situation I secretly felt she had created by not taking care of things earlier. Initially she didn't have enough insurance to cover everything, so that gave me the way to go into fix-it mode. "If money is the only thing standing between life and death," I told her, "we're gonna get the fucking money."

I desperately thought I could save her life. You want to get into Sloan Kettering? Hold on, let me call my publicist and make sure you get in to see the doctors at Sloan Kettering. The Young Survivor Coalition looked like the best organization connecting young women with resources and a path to life, so we were gonna go all in with the YSC. I would become their best celebrity friend. If we had the right amount of money, the right amount of connections, the right amount of networking, then we could beat it. Why else was I famous?

I threw myself into advocacy, hosting small seminars to promote the importance of prioritizing your own health. I used the analogy that they use when you're getting on the plane. "You've got to put your mask on before you help anybody else," I said countless times. "If you prioritize yourself, you're gonna save yourself."

In interviews, I would bring it up constantly.

"Is Will Smith a good kisser?"

"You bet he is," I'd say, "and you know you can bet your life on early detection. Did you know that eleven thousand women under forty are diagnosed with breast cancer every year?"

Susan G. Komen made me a Circle of Promise Ambassador, then a Global Ambassador. In 2008 they sent me to Kumasi, Ghana, to help dedicate the country's first breast health facility, one of the only ones in West Africa. I wanted to bring to the world the message that breast cancer is treatable and survivable.

One of the speakers that day was Dr. Lisa Newman, an African American surgical oncologist out of the University of Michigan. She was talking about what people can expect as far as prognosis.

When I heard her say the word "metastatic," my ears perked

up. That was Sook's diagnosis. It's funny, I thought, I never really knew what "metastatic" meant.

And then I learned.

"Of course," Dr. Newman said, "there is no cure for metastatic breast cancer."

Everything else was drowned out, and I heard her words as an echo. "There is no cure for metastatic breast cancer." But wait. We've got the money. We are seeing the best doctors. We are doing all this work. What do you mean?

Then it all became very clear to me: Sook was gonna die, no matter what we did. There is no cure for metastatic breast cancer. This was three years into Sookie's journey—a sister should have read up on "metastatic" at this point. I definitely shouldn't have been sitting there in Ghana, on the other side of the world from my dear friend, finding out that she was going to die no matter how much I gamed the system.

It was like that moment in the living room with Ray. I was the last to understand the truth I didn't want to accept. Clueless Nickie, thinking she knew what was best for everyone.

FOR RAY AND ME, LIFE BECAME ABOUT TRYING TO SPEND AS MUCH TIME AS possible with Sook. She was still going full speed ahead, lobbying in D.C. and still trying to get into clinical trials for treatment. She got a great boyfriend and a dog. She had hope, but she was very clear that it was more about buying time than finding a cure. The thing that she was excited about was that while she was getting a few more months from the latest clinical trial, what they were learning from her would help other women.

On one of her better days, I was in New York for some work

event. We met down in SoHo at this restaurant, at a time when we knew it would be empty. We just wanted to be girlfriends.

We held hands, and literally as I was asking her what she wanted her legacy to be, what she wanted me to carry on, I felt someone standing next to our table.

"I never do this . . ." she said.

She was a tall woman, well dressed and looking like she knew better.

I turned. "I am so sorry," I said. "This is not a good time."

"This is just going to take a second," she said.

Sook wouldn't look at her. Finally, I turned to the woman and smiled. I chose to satiate this woman's need, just to make her go away.

It was a minute, maybe a minute and a half with Sook that I wouldn't get back. I returned to Sook and again asked her what she wanted her legacy to be. What message she wanted me to carry on.

"I want you to tell people that fear can kill you," Sook said. "I was afraid, and it killed me."

It was my last lunch with Sook.

RAY CALLED ME NEAR THE END OF THE SECOND WEEK OF JUNE 2010. "Look, it's coming," he said. "If you want to be able to talk to Sook while she is able to respond, you should come now."

I booked a flight to spend the weekend with her in New York. Then I got a call from one of the execs behind *Jumping the Broom.* They really liked me for one of the starring roles, but they had a concern about a false tabloid report that I had torn apart Dwyane's marriage. One of the producers was megapastor T. D.

Jakes, and if I didn't go to a meeting on Friday, I wasn't going to get the part. I made the decision to go. I delayed my flight to get in Saturday morning.

The meeting boiled down to "Will Christian women go to see a movie starring a supposed home-wrecker?" I so wanted people to like me, to choose me, that I was putting aside a very real situation that demanded my immediate presence.

These people knew the situation with Sookie. My friend was across the country dying, and they were still asking me if I was a good enough Christian to sell tickets. I could have had another day with her or even just a few more hours if I hadn't had to convince people I am a good person. I didn't even get the part, and to this day, I regret nothing more than taking that meeting and trying to explain gossip. Rumors that were easily proven false, but why let a little thing like the truth get in the way of a good lie? But I was so stuck in wanting people to like me that I went to the meeting before I got on the plane. Just to try to plead my case to producers and an executive that I was not this home-wrecker described by people who had absolutely no real information about the situation.

When I finally got to Sookie's apartment, Ray met me outside. He tried to prepare me before I walked in.

"It's bad, Nickie," he said. "We've all been on shifts. She wants to die at home."

When I walked in, you could smell death. Decay. I will never forget it. The nurses had transformed her apartment, once this cute little bachelorette pad, into a home hospice. Sook's boyfriend was there, as was her whole family: her mom, her older brother Sam, and her two sisters. Her dad had driven up from New Jersey. And at the center was Sook, in a hospital bed they'd brought in.

"I'm sorry it smells really bad in here," she said.

"It does, actually."

"I wish some of our relationships gave off this smell," she joked. "We'd have known they were over."

"Catch a whiff," I said, "and 'Whoo, see ya.'"

What I loved most was when she said out of nowhere, "Will *somebody* go and get me some hair removal cream?" A side effect of one of her meds was hair growth, and she was getting a mustache. Her sisters were there painting her nails, trying to make her feel as pretty as possible. I was ready to have deep conversations about life and death, but she wanted nothing to do with that. So I gave up control and allowed Sook to lead me.

"I want to talk about the Kardashians," she said. That was Sook, a girls' girl to the end.

Ray joined us, and Sook and I entertained her sisters with stories of growing up in Pleasanton. We laughed about the guys we loved from After Dark, and I told the girls the tales of Little Screw and my Greek-Mexican beauty school dropout. Ray mimed how to jump-start the family Studebaker, and their mom pretended to be shocked at how often we'd done it.

At the end, we are our stories, some shared and some lived alone. I wanted nothing more than for Sook's story to have a happy ending.

She made it to that Wednesday, five years into her diagnosis. I won't turn her into Susan B. Anthony, but she definitely wanted people to prioritize themselves and their health and not to be afraid of going to the doctor. To always get a few opinions and try to live your best life. She didn't want the conversation or our advocacy work to die with her. It couldn't be that Ray and I became breast health advocates to save Sookie, but if we couldn't help Sook, to hell with everyone else. She didn't want that. To this day, I do what my schedule allows, and I am very active in supporting Planned Parenthood. They offer low- and no-cost breast health care, and for a lot of people, Planned Parenthood is the only time they see a doctor. And I always try to incorporate health and wellness anytime I'm speaking, because now it just comes up naturally.

Ray has the longest-running relationship of anyone that I know. He and his partner have a country home in Connecticut—the whole nine yards. As I was writing this I could always text Ray to make sure I had the details down correctly.

And so, *you,* my sweet, patient, understanding reader: Sookie made me promise to tell you not to act out of fear. I can only add that you can be scared to death, as I've been while sharing these stories with you, and do the thing you need to do anyway.

Take care of yourself.

acknowledgments

I want to thank the people of Dey Street Books and HarperCollins Publishers. Thanks especially to my editor, Carrie Thornton, for her help in bringing this book to the world.

Also to Sean Newcott, Ploy Siripant, Ben Steinberg, Kendra Newton, Heidi Richter, and Lynn Grady.

Thanks to Albert Lee for encouraging me to write a book. And to Kevin Carr O'Leary, for hearing my words and making them sing.

To my manager and enabler Jeff Morrone, the longest, most productive relationship I've ever had. Thank you for believing in me. I am grateful for your vision, and your tireless efforts to help make my dreams a reality.

I also want to thank Holly Shakoor and Stephanie Durning, Patti Felker, Brad Rose, David Guillod, and Todd Shuster for advocating for me. They are the people you want in your corner.

Thank you to my uncle, James Francis Glass, for being the perfect godfather. One who encouraged shenanigans and wacky inappropriate hijinks. And doing it all unapologetically.

Thank you to the people who acknowledge turn signals and let people in. You are the real MVPs.

To my mom, thank you for your love and respect of words, books, and safe learning spaces. You created distant galaxies in a brain hardwired to stay grounded on Earth. Thank you.

Dad, thank you for showing me that real change is possible at any age, and that it's never too late to evolve and live your best life.

To my sisters, thank you for loving me and supporting me. And always letting me be Deena Jones during Christmas sing-alongs.

To the boys, I know I'm gone a lot but I hope that during my absences I am making you proud. Thank you for always having my back and being my protectors.

To my poopy, D . . . Thank you for waking me up with that smile and positive vibes every morning and making me feel invincible and loved completely.

about the author

Gabrielle Union is an actress and activist. Currently she stars as the titular character in the critically acclaimed drama *Being Mary Jane* on BET. She is an outspoken activist for women's reproductive health and victims of sexual assault. She lives in Miami, Florida.